Steven Welfare
My Lyrics

I

My looping is phenomenal, I will admit,
vinyl or digital, even scratch a bit.
Besides the main frontline incentives are
lit, essential enthusiasm, now it is my
mind that is hit.
Big time! I know everybody wonders
what it's like at the top, I ain't never
going to drop.

With the force of a vice, I don't tell you twice, I don't think that I'm going to cause living is nice.
But who do I dream of? Ain't that a plain. Superior scenario, who needs that fame?
It's what I have at the minute my spacing a game, changing again
Like feelings inside running insane. I keep to a standard it's wicked I came.
I Love to cane, whose kidding? In this life we're already to blame.

Giving up an antidote, I can never spell, meanings of words just collide
You're going to understand quite well
Girls spinning round in my head fewer brain cells is what I'm left with.
I'm not trying to go too fast, just understand the last path. Taste, you've got to have tactics,
I see in life that with no Love there'd be no magic, Like a hat trick.

A formulation is what people need, I
can provide the bassline, rhythms
bleed.
I've got to be wondering cause I'm in
demand, Want to get with this, I must
take a stand.
Like I said before, there are not any
flaws, Miracles in a sandstorm just
avoiding the war.
Big up, I quote like direct the next door,
why did you come here for?
Questions of a serious case I don't
always face right away I'm trying to
relax, learn why.
And then I may carry on with my
recital, mental, vital I live a life of tidal
qualities finally in the mix
Easy for a dj there ain't nothing I can't
fix as I pick brand new classics on my
feet wear ticks.

Dazed, amazed it took me a while to
get down with the craze
Annoyed? I always knew I could play,
since back in the day,

But here in the future I've lots more to say.
Beautiful bodies rule my life
This is my secret and it isn't right to go backwards on me, a finer emcee,
I'm raving the industry, I'm lucky that it's me.
Backwards in the street, is it just my eyes or just my ears?
I may fantasize but I've got my fears,
Too many, too near, I wonder
Keep a score in Heaven, I can't imagine going under.
Cause when I'm up, a brand new level, melodies written,
You know that I'm able to back labels with consciousness,
Basslines with treble, meeting other people the complete cyber pebble.

Scoring I style, scenario I create out to keep you up to date with

The infinite lines you need as you
gyrate.
Life, an incredible score to live, lucky
you have the gift.
I'll give you a rise you could call it a lift
cause
I like to drive you
Why not admit? Never down a top
buzz is it.
Now I've learnt to live with a feeling so
clear,
Not too dear as I charge on escalating
with no fear.
A sky cycle my head is an item.
Correct use of lingo leads me to be
lighting the path,
Hallway, I can't remember, another
doorway? You do it your way.
January to December, tracks in a row,
Techno in the summer, techno in the
snow,
Jungle techno is just one way to go.
We'll never give it up, it's all you have to
know.

Dancing on the virtual tip, give your friends that hip hop trip.

When they hear, I'm never going to slip, On the turntables I can play quick. For all your dreams and simpler things, Into the present. I've got to mention, it's my intention to try
As I'm trying out this sonic invention. I've seen what I've brought so casual like a dream, together extending through my thoughts
The only ending the ones that I see, across my stone cold glossary, a manual.

Full of words that will frazzle any feeling of loss behind me no boss, I'm starting Basically financially. Tonight, not only what I bought is down to me.
How many ways to pay old school guarded mysteries.
I'm in a field and can play headphones are my best sign for me to show away.

To front a font today. New Age design no time decay.

By myself am I the only one who understands reality?
Breaking it down in the heart pled heartfelt energy
Alternatively through life to which there are keys we can find our indescribable ways.
So many. The noise is here like a cartographers map. Never undesirable always vital such as air.
In front of the crowd I'm going to say I care for more sublime controls I rap.
Questions in the English language answers in original text form
Traditional I get warm confronting that which is black.
Steady is my hand like my mind... On the attack.

Yes, my gangsters home, caught him at this pace

Coming quicker than a roller coaster as I deliver the bass

Clever stuff, never rough, never giving up, I'm going to be tough.

This fuss. TV, radio anything else that is clear

Beyond your thought or memory raving is something near

So sometimes I am wrong, easy to recite incidental with flair

Because I'm nice, you'll never have to think twice

With production, coordination and flavour

I think I catch the air as a cool fresh explanation.

My latest invention is too bad in equivalent to new stacks

Takes my time as I breathe and is my exposure. Never told you

But novelty is sometimes period. I forget my nerve

I'm forgetting love if I let it loose I'm going to swerve.

Oh you must believe, like air I'll be gentle with a movement now that's elemental
Too late now is it, to late to see? With an international style
Commended virtually here for all beginners cause I've found identity.
Difficult, don't mean to be anarchic, but I see and should realise
That there's some scenery over this, not to deceive, but to deliver
As your body gives a shiver, quicker with my voice cause the words are getting bigger.
Figure, like an equation or a multiple chance to get back to the dance as critical as an advance
Paid, like a miracle, played so satirical yes I'm believable.

Super seder credible scribbler on with the slate cause it's great my lyrical fate
Fold and create for the future it's weight that I include confirmed as

A prodigy, a paradox, a passing through time, a trinity, a mystery, the "I know it's fine"
Too rude? Interlude with another line inevitable no evil dead calm
No foul from me as I deliver from harm.
Long live the valleys that impress me; down with momentum and into their key.

Light will save every passionate emcee, hated by the nation or just fashioned by me.
Cause yes when I come I chill to come correct, the ideal world around my neck.

True confessions of the past, a designer blast, holding onto something that's not holding onto me.
So far as I can touch my identity be false never and arrange to profess.
Casual nostalgia is nothing less now the music's changed let's see what's the best.

Laying down a new style cause I can
see I'm fresh, never wrecked
Legitimate in only present tense, fibre
fine technology you can feel the sense.

Realms realistic, spinning every
adjective, the trouble in my life won't be
gone over night.
My morals selective, touching the rim of
unconsciousness like a nail in a rock.
Rushing over the shock, I'm into play
reality cause nature has it's knock.
Reckoning like time, to stay ahead of
the flock.
I don't know what else I can say now,
are you into the plot? I'm glad I never
loose it.
I might loose what I've got, I always find
a shot to speak like the perfect host
A story on the boil I try to carry on, I
know I'll never spoil.

Taking force, I only hope the mic can
understand me spending time with the
physical operand

Dropping them facts like a tool we can rewind, play with, they're too cool.
Upto us this future is dawning a real root, radical to suit
Built from a past which at best stayed mute we can have a louder future, ain't that cute?
Bilingual basic melody kicking back although there is no enemy
Stereo and so virtual I need that touch to leave me certain
Rapology the way to explain hidden and complex the rules, managing is my game.
Now you know my name. And things are not the same
A new style to write with though I'm changing every lane
Biased before I decide easy to recall my brain. Lyrics very necessary so that I fulfil the cane.
It's mostly the same as I trip on, trip out I could find myself. See. I am never in doubt.

The rules of rap, it seems so elemental but now when I look back:
More than coincidental had to write it down.
Starting with a parcel of the way things are in my town. Where I live. I've got to give
A message to the others as a sign they can receive Knowledge I'm surely releasing mixing music
Folding and creasing. Always on the beats cause I'm going to blow your mind, no tease.
My messages continue, out to break repetitive flow calm to my lingo
That's the way my thing goes alphabet connecting where didn't all the time go.
How are we sounding now, you know that I can double?
In any rhyme of any length, hip hop ain't no trouble.
My fluid sense is from electric friends I can always cause a bubble.

Trip hop hanging like a floating balloon, ballast rejected could level to the moon. I come across with no fear as a time hits severe, knowledge too much for those in peer.

Why do I feel like I've lived a life before, experience and visions the feeling is raw.

Into and over we haven't a flaw. Onto and conclude with an innocent curfew. I'd stop before I hurt you, undercover I confess, take a back seat in my test. When we speak the same language for our guidance we are blessed.

Who am I? I must ask myself before I loose my learning. Take the call for hardcore.

Honest as I drop the beats, brains, I know with force deranged.

Harmonies come from space through the dances pre-ordained.

Spending complete observation with the trance, a new foundation

Records in motion, formulation, the
starting of a creation.
Bass boy handle the pitch if your fingers
want to scratch give the records an itch
I survive to strive on the mix faults never
flattering, mistakes I fix.
Come quick if you decide, I'll put you
on a ride subtle, the game of technique
that never lies
Sliding focus, intensify playing up the
rave game until the day that I die.
Kick-back from the strength of too fly
loosing no battles and I always know
why.
History has the flow as the pieces add-
up, synchronisation?
The method of my hardcore narration
blown to bits, an undue dedication?
Satisfaction guaranteed we all need
salvation.

My manner runs clear, a smooth
occupation
Into your frequency
A new celebration

Into your soul, a new destination.
Comprehension, intervention
Turning my words round to show my
intention
An extension of modest modulation
Big up my fine dictation. Major
selection.
Is it safe to be proud or what? With so
much virtual
I'd felt hurt, but now I realise. What I
do? Like a game of chess.
Maybe too modest I confess, a cool
place to start, a king, a queen,
Pieces from my heart so what's moving
next?
Graphical text. Confounded I progress,
records requested reviewed.
Remind me of a time where I'm mostly
a guest.
Shot to bits with a tune, by a state,
infrasonic melody a symmetrical quest.

I know where I am, control an entire
mix, sliding, rewinding.

Until I reach what'll stretch. Not short of
the truth and I'm here with the rest of it.
Lines we'll be crossing until I get
confused, too bad to get right, delicate I
choose.
Magnetic, no cold dialect, in a
language called English what could go
wrong?
On account of the first lines I'm into a
song. Forces alive!
Feel the five, my only sixth is
conveyance of a matrix.
Is it any good I've got to know. Not too
big or too small.
My enemies fall, chaotic like bankrupt
your dj with a fine top.
Area is suggestive finally a back drop. A
social behaviour I won't slop.
I know I'm in a managerial position as I
wait for this vital collision.
Secrets attributed to the sun, retribution
of the stars.
Telepathy and success, intelligence is
granted I hope we all make it...

You might like my concept. But don't just glance. My romance, I am never going to stop.
With a hip hop connection the jungle underground will rock.
Is it an infinite task to get in with the past?
The lines that I don't need, can still tease, precious to read, only myself now a believer.

No secret that I can be worried, my writing's scurried,
Way down to the nitty gritty but not hurried.

Multiple rational in a life that's blurred, cool elementally, energy a burst.
Aurally coherent audibly reversible, like a burst bubble
Here to cause trouble. With a beginning a middle and an end.
Not aiming to loose friends an adverse coefficient can't pretend

To be what you don't see,
harmoniously, naturally is my proficient
Aid that comes to me.
Signs enormous, imagine.
The freshest dance code, the latest
dance key.
If I can say a ritual that will take your
pain away it's like a planet to play on,
With a loaded expedition calm as we
display on-intensions unknown.
My philosophy don't drown as I cut
down with the facts, don't so many
wear the crown?
No bloated invitation, I'm not green, so
follow me a new emcee.
Yes like a baby drive me sanely crazy
I'm no foreign policy I might want you
to race me.
I need advice on thinking twice,
seconded by my memory, lateral
dimensions such shapes I can see
Don't step away. You shouldn't fear
what may take your life over , nova-
decay.

So this is where I set a level straight, clear.
Harmonious as a tear.

I only dream and ask questions of these dimensions so tremendous I fill you with feeling sincere.
Looked at where to start
I had a heart. A higher function could just lead us all apart.
Taught to follow signs as in a modern world we change
How to challenge what you say and what you hear is not so strange.
I feel I've lost a bad thing it's gone as is said, it's funny with no
Patterns to hold me down gives me colours more
Silent like a needle tip I'm into talking raw
Now I live with the truth nothing is sore, cause I am hardcore.
As you hear my dj progress I'm only back with the best

Lyrics aimed to soothe you and a tune
that will congress.
We're talking inter-frame mixing voices
that you need.

Kick drums sophisticated yes I lead the
score, atomic in overture like a cruise
missile to the core.
I'm not bad I tell my luck locks sane
Now I'm out of preaching that we're all
in the game.
I've been with runaways, hardcore,
people into rave
Faces I will save as I give away.
Wicked so many vice, do I have to think
twice to convey my sense
I only mean what I meant, versions
around me are stranded when
Virtually we can see through the
screen,
Purposeful belief will lead to the dream.
Lyrics with a warning, always more
than what they seem.
Coherent melody twisting words into
passed what left you behind my last

Catch, coherent lyrics yes here I write a
stack. Leaving profits below.
You're only in the know and I am
jealous so I attack as I give flow.

Sane pretence my get up never slow
with my words they're going to go.
Alphabet apocalypse this time turning
your world into snow.
Careful as I cover, uncover an
underground series
Undercover of my mind a raver in relay
I will find
Any loop to tell you the way I choose a
new grind.

Bassline chaotic, I'm into the plot into a
darkland that is forgotten.
I might make you bite my lines so I'm
set with advanced effect.
It's like a tip now that I'm older so for
the chip, know that I told you.
It is not obvious, but I won't curse you.
I've got money making money though I
lie it ain't a lot.

I'm into the code that we're making,
patterns I'm taking, secret screens on a
battle field not faking.
Let me take you to places that are not
far.
Colourful grammatic cross the line I am
an art.
I'm only finding some great new
reasons to start.
I like to stay in operation cause I have a
part.
Reasons cater for more lines narrative as
I portrait to you.
Won't leave you late it's pure I have a
heart,
I'm mostly writing about now, like the
time is and how.
After war and revolution, you can study
mass volition, a million missions
And so many, many millions of people.
Mostly and I hold hope
That we're all together so you can hear
every note rhythmically square.
Thanks for using the power, your vote
taking this medium.

Correct I call you secure. Probably
better for newer.
Information passing my lips, easy to skip
over what is under.
Reverse my lines and recall like thunder
any number.
In my mind is a fence, like a breeze may
event
Clever how I'm knowing are you seeing
what I meant? Music calls for me.

Pop. Only an idea in the dealers mind.
He knows his points
As he sells to his kind taking musical
feelings not noting their ambition
New profit to himself but where did it
start? In a beginning
An ounce, a quarter or a key reflected
dog tag images flicker through TV.
A radio his mind searching for answers
romance a machine
Feeling for the knowledge of control,
the knowledge as is learnt
Is never left in the dirt, the flower
blooms in a time to assume

Not any stunts just dereliction of all false front. Concerned for viewers an idea that is blunt.

He wants to stay in the front at the brink, too quick to think,
reconsideration you love to feel the link Hot as inferno changing what into things. Ok that I'm like this it is just what my luck brings.
How many rhymes cease to explain my currency of lingo, adjectivally talking Warning. Speaking I'm warning,
glowing, transmitting energy warming. Truly storming, how else can I tell myself what is a good thing
For the latest scene, I assume like a king. Too diverse to tell you what it means. What you don't know are the colours at my side, big as necessary, don't you know I like to ride?
If I am a fool then what could I decide? How to live hot to dream is all for me to find.

Rhythm is our structure on basic hardcore ground, these are my morals of which I am so proud.

I feel like I must do this, God told me to play them loud.

While I scratch I overload with energy, electricity is the catch.

I watch out cause I'm rare, earlier lost then no despair, back with a reason if I dare.

I can tell the truth I am dark, commissioned to myself, earning safer salaries

Inducing techno boundaries, dance to death our standards, jungle no moral myth.

It is so difficult now, life with it's voices, my element performing an emcee takes his choices.

I can hear if only I believe, back on the circuit a message to achieve.

Closing angles, narrowing blips, maybe I can mention I hope my life is a hit

Basically instinct I can lead to many places mostly as I trust lasers and tracers.
Patterns of solitude enter my head as vision is filled with all that I have said.
Working out brief encounters of a plan, divisible fashion I'm not denying
That I can open up procedures at will. I pay the bill to get ill.

Formulae guys and people looking only out for their family
The meals that they're cooking, their individuality, who am I
You may ask to even examine their paths. But life is a blast, it's not the only way
But as a subject is passed, the impossible subject cause it's impossible
Just to glance back when the way that my life has advanced.
Is as quick as a panther, a python. A calculator for when my life is saying see you later

Controlling memories, dreams and the sound that I hear so what can I do? Motion in frames, talking in games, not living so tame.

My fast lane is audio justice my thoughts are just wicked again. Touch this peaceful as the plain, I try to stay out of trouble, it's less of a strain.

Living is our nature but is life our only course?
I like to drop a beat like a core through the future that I saw.
Like a new plot, my libido a micro dot.

I wake up, light the first cigarette of the day I try to smoke away my worries but with my sleep I pay.
Another day has passed and left me on my way. How can I miss the one I love so much?
I try. She ain't here. In my life sadly missing, I am listening to music, an architectural thing

Everyday it might cross my mind, but I have been left with a bassline, am I so unkind?

Do I tend to forget? Don't want to loose my set.

In a higher place I like to be following myself as my emcee. Unique prodigy, cosmic rhapsody.

When words are in the right places you can follow me. I ain't so bad, my life tells me that

I can really turn it out, up when I want to laugh.

But now what can I say when in my way, in my path

Are a million words, faces that don't knock me out of phase.

It's nice to get even but nicer to leave them

People that don't believe when with the hype I am an achiever.

II

How low can people go it will amaze
me, I got so depressed it put me in a
daze,

Weeks pass months and days, I own
this lyrical phase,

Although the really big questions are
hidden in a maze.

I'll stay discreet which round here is
neat. Hip hop hardcore reckons and a
duty that I beat.

So out my further feelings since I've
been revealing

You're out of control, it's breath that
you'll be needing, why tar me cause
your so tame?

Why play me? I'm not your little game, I
see the present, it only seems to lie,

A wicked device to evoke alibi.

Everybody has an advantage over me, I
feel watched, my chemistry,

Fools below me, fuel is the key, when you've somebody to talk to it sets your spirit free.

Annoyed now within kinetic energy, what glitches done to me.

Although I set the evening in swing it is a bad hall beat that I bring.

I am jealous when there is no love at my side,

Cause I've seen life's far side, at least my friends are in control, I double up with the flow.

Future sound for the future sound keep moving

Let's keep minimal my mind not mimicking a sound to decipher.

Cause I'm sharp like a sniper just wondering whether to arm myself with all, aim myself at all.

At all cause I'm forgetting finales, on the future sound I'm brighter.

Got to be aware, hypnotising feelings I thought I knew the score,

Often setting a zone, a game, you know I came, to at least let

You know, pure harmonious quantities that really care.

Future sound on the future sound I'm talking
Now with a miracle thought it's just the future that I'm wondering.
Stalling? Still calling on the future sound a dawning.
Concerned, but to this day I draw a key.
Dimensions displaced graphically
Know how determined synonymously
I earn what I use, burn my own hardcore fuse,
I'm like a bomb so just don't get confused.
Early I am a charm so you don't stop
Music says anything and into the dream shop.

The lapse. No lapse, raging on attack filling in infinity like Santa fills his sack.
Back to the track the future never lies
Writing this as lyrics helps the buzz intensify.

Wise, writing this is making me bright.
Why wrestle with the light when
there's no need to fight?
Quite, I light another candle in this
game create a sight.
That maybe or, might just move you
Calming facility that is boundless.

Clever as I unwind, though trying hard
to impress.
Enough said. I can't pretend I am a
friend
Rocking in the jungle, cause jungle is a
trend.
Judge me on my morals cause my
morals I will send. Pretending only
never
that I'm better now than then.
Now and again. Appearing like I never
end
Am I charm less or harmless, sure or just
on form?
Together, to and from, to and throw
You ought to know, this is the message.
How did it go?

33

It's no worse, words. Abusive adverbs in the right places aren't no curse.

I've rehearsed it's a new day sometimes my thought is in verse.

Is it my duty, though I love to deliver techno beauty

My heart is the chords, notes, if you have it you can quote me.

Specifically a motion that will float

I'm now going to boast but kids are into cyber sonics from coast to coast.

It is the most, but now I'm getting fluid I feel like a ghost.

Ancient, I'm honest my life like a post.

I am the host to a familiar feeling that is life,

Everyday my actions may play, information I have to decipher, functions.

Economic structure that grows on what is nice as the days pass like nights.

No trouble to be quite right.

Sometimes we have fun, recollection of memories smoking in the sun. Shine,

light high time never too late. Myself I
never underestimate.
The power of what I rate, any positive
form is great.
This is from the unique master of a slate.
Clever, I'll be falling through
mathematics I create.
Instamatic fate, automatic from a raver
Whose behaviour is quick as the flash
on a camera
No stammer, can you understand just
what I have in my hands to this date,
milder manner.
Since now I'm across the board
I'm as fixed as a banner.
So thanks to my mind, I nearly forgot, it
took a friend to tell me, that I admire
So much. More than just a touch
moving in the right direction, is it
without detection?
Dedication, what I see is true, the
sometimes vital normal figures out
fortune. Basslines no torture.

My last chapter got me over with
scripture really right honestly tight if
phrase is
My language, it pays to play bright.
With the information flowing through
the
Mixing of the night. I'm still note for
note not narrow like a boat, thin like
A cobra, be pleased that I told you.
Exposing like a ministry the jobs that we
do, in the social infrastructure,
We all have our lanes, all choose our
news. The future fairly said
Can hold a lot of beauty, although
memories we loose. The sky like the sea
is blue
Living everyday until our lives are
through.
Now sometimes I've been down but
you've just got to recognise what I do.
Earn the pounds to socialise and play
the games that are true. I can know
My self tell it not to get confused,
I'll just stay inside myself and hope I'm
happy soon.

I'm mixed, I've got a phantom. Too hardcore than you'd care to fathom. I'm in the deep cause I'm not short of stamina. Don't get offended by this rapping seminar.

Handling all, buzzing our time, seeing through things inventing rhyme. Minutes to get laced, in with a bad craze, why waste this pace.
I can consume miraculous space as I read and I trace, foretelling language In a race like pattern and form. I've heard that you would like this all hardcore.
Techno, ambience for life. I may slow down to consume what is nice.

The techno path would not be living without vice just good advice, two djs. What has got me concerned it's since it is nowadays who knows crime pays? But this is just not right, justice is a hot rock, every criminals back drop.

At times my journey has narrowed I'm only stable, I never fall only clear to other players at all.

Opening predictions design above all function, seeking self determined

Product, orientation specific terrific, exploding technicolour

Although versions I could offer to my brother.

Seconds to construct, I take my time as I instruct

Basic phenomenal linguistic headstrong rush.

Delicately worded is my game, frame by frame

I'm never similar to the other class of emcee, compared to me so many are lame.

Vain, here I'm very satirical, but not one is my mother, we've never been joined by umbilical cord, call me a brother.

I may be the last, fastest, it's a blast, time for another.

Run right in a circle, never suffer, up above my mind is rougher.

Together I never fall affray of what I
utter
Cause I'm so clever I let them think that
I'm a nutter
Anyway, besides the clause I state there
ain't no other.
Hotter, like water I boil, my style will
never spoil
Always down from me fresh as I profile,
tougher
Writing for a life that's as vivid as I am
versatile.
With the sounds of my voice
Setting a boundary we work the
ground.
On the slip now take a trip on how my
history is the right circuit.
Beyond control? Well no, not mine,
well equipped feeling fine.
I've got to learn from what I write as
well as I hear. Not trying to get over
Any mind barrier thought flux or fear
anticipated my past disappears.
Sometimes I've got to take time,
rehearsal really necessary.

Examination of my essay as an
understudy recalling
What will make you worry.
Fascinating bassline moves me into
trouble,
As I witness things and motions,
collectively I've noted - time to
comprehend.
Versions of a story that will never end.
My poetic symphony, an emcee
journeys trend.
Maximum facts never in a muddle
sober for a second.
The largest mysteries I reckon, checking
Their score like a reflection, is my
intention
Hardcore truth is reality not invention.
Still, she is seeing over me, insight
played by her mind which is so right
The ladies in my life dj this effect in my
life is just one sweet way.
Synchronising enemy keyed
throughout the day I'm kicking virtual
melodies in a pattern with a sway

Cautious of my form, in life you've got to pray.
On top of imagination my style with no decay. Coming now closer,
harmonic footsteps away
I always like to notice I've a thought that can stay
Into the feeling steadily between the lines revealing no conceding.

In a way I've so many things to say, to the point, you know the sky's the limit
No science fiction, if this is a story then I'm in it
Narrowing my margins, they're lines that are specific.
Not empty, a fund, in front of my massive
Break up and around the disc jockey style
Vibes that are never sarcastic, jungle article sound
Built for the future from a past that pounds.

Moving on, not loosing what I choose, into any episode like news kicks it's views.

Not really a lie it is old father time's alibi, you've got to understand that I try. Basically foresight has led me to a gap of peace that I use for release Technology high tech as digital as any fest I can describe in detail the beast.

Designing deciding the multi core I'm only sane.

Not bothered by the catch, they're never one to lie.

How can I say yes while I'm wondering what's best.

Why? What will watch, induced upon I am the boss.

Close decent scenes form an animation dream.

Always into a new game or the latest, jet set to my head and we relate.

Backed up are feelings that I can create. Twains thy sight may never meet my brother.

My mind, just feeling immaculate, any thought that I have
Just my own, looking back at a sense finale. In a field I take it all alone.
Pride in me will never cause a frown, I'll never worry
When I'm down, although. Sounds I've found explain if I hurry
Sounds explain I've found a new sound. Time to change as only time unfolds
Understanding anything understand my written word. Everything is delicate as understood what is observed.
I'm always moving like the fire, intimate. Reassuringly passive I just pass you with this knack
It's vital coordination leaves my body intact
What I find is a fact, all our interests Invested line up and groove like lines on a map
I improve as the speaker takes up the slack

Modulation of knowledge down on a track.
Finely filtered my idea tonight burning bright in the back of an emcees mind.
My destiny of voyage not out of place to narrate like foliage.
The jungle beginning from a wars end. That old rave trend. It is important to think.
Alignment is what I send no pick and mix on with heavy justice I won't transfix you. Take a breath.
The way to me a record is released is such a fleece
The best of some only stay at the top for a few days
Tastes and flavours alter my memories, disco disciple. Dancing with lyrical melodies now is the score.
Laced chained to the ground where I found more
Pop is an attitude which for the masses can forge correctness.
Over the years studio techniques have lead to

Now I'm hectic, to drop ink, everything that I think. Before you blink, we're at the next link.

Broadened horizons here display now trouble, new terms to come to deal with on the double.
Borders that show fine art illustration of mass political global mediation.
This is my latest translation. No invention, it's my creation.
Youth, that's what the universe is about and here's the proof
My secret is I always knew that my mixing is the truth.
Times I've spent trying to change in the past I nearly went insane
Until I realised what's said is gone we'll live for tomorrow.
The past where we're from. Now is the perfect foundation to make friends
Design trends, time is an analogy my past all rapology.

Simple sophistication synthetic with style, sometimes I wish that I weren't prophetic
Now that I've seen you I cannot be rejected
So I don't cease to smile, only corrected energy respected.
I guess you could argue but why bother against me I am big brother with a tangent to be seen in
My restless melody won't let you be deceived, this is what we should believe in.
My lines on the paper are dope I hope that my rhythms are virtuous.
Wise to this yet you must have rehearsed your ears.
I'm back across with reasons provoked through years. The burning seers.

I remember to bring my pen down, at least now I can't change the past
The future is opposite and gives us all a place to go, where no one knows.

Tastefully deciding how I'm going to take the next blow, blast.

Figuring fast, coordinating structure with a chemical founding.

Through the roughest minutes, seconds have been pounding.

Because I'm the lyrical master on the ground.

Easy to rap any hip fact around, I stay with feeling,

That is assured to be keeping me down.

I don't wear out, I'm always on time

Not messing with your lives just living mine. I fly through function

Now I'm back with the catch as I'm flaunting the action.

Seen on the rewind, the future faction.

Just a fraction away from kicking

You have been listening to what this emcee has been picking

Reality, love is life, next time I'll be back with a tongue like a knife.

I'll try what I can, there ain't a finer plan in existence

Our impedance bringing us together is
the proof
Profiles in the light scoop the truth, bad
messages from the past
Is an escape, the future always does
relate
So I'm a blast, check the catch, it's not
the last.
Plain to remind I find I'm just the same
again.
Building on a premise from a hall of
fame.
Bad through to the future still
remaining kind
See I've been through blind, fall on
death ears, sometimes
I recollect through my past times. New
fears.
Dealing with the new clear, now
nothing is unclear
I collect so many well named rhymes,
specific signs,
And spend time inside a well designed
mind
Groomed, fine tuned, controlled.

Can you relate to this, it's my decision
Humanity collision, is destiny a dream?
I'll stay on top of fortune with
conditional routine.
Midnight, there ain't much doing but
I'm working hard just got to keep
screwing.
Do I achieve it might be argued I could
question but now I'm luring,
The question of time, the way I spend it,
the fabric of dilution.
By standing I'm absolute, stating
intentions into my mind is my sonic
invention.
An adult joke at an adult time, it's
relationship to me is how I'm going to
skit
When I'm on my own I rave my scores,
all my time to give, it's like a fire I've lit.
I'm nimble like my pen to paper real I'm
what you take
The choice is yours my anticipation is
clear in stakes.

Educating, yes right here intoxicating mesmerising I plan to be down with what is relating.

That which is known I may have thrown folly into reason, without any other.

Is my rhyme in season? I wouldn't be a brother if I couldn't be teasing.

Tracks with one another, testing what is lesser, what is greater.

Whoever's with that fader is no guesser. Portrayer of the future, now.

Cause we're all on one side of the wall, we have all got to bother, are we convincing one another?

I might learn a new rule but you I will not smother we will survive, enhancing energy

Spoken, speaking sense revealing melodic dance key I'll be resetting a mystery.

I'm a standard so I've wondered statistics leave me they're never bonded

And some beyond any false reasons
doubt will leave you screaming.
Confusing;
Memories are a deity like dreams, I'm
confessing a new remedy;
Beckoning hyphenated strategies
imposing identity for a heart felt sanity.
Give able, like the force I think I gave
understandable is what we may create.
I try to find out what I'm like, I'm no
closer. An urban traveller in my dreams,
Small snatches real, so on the other side
what seems like another time.
We're into delicate decision and raw no
opposition to the questions just no flaw.
Are there any rules, you must have
heard it before
I've come back from the creator only
knowing hardcore.
Wish it could stay that way, what am I
trying to say forecast a list of reasons to
see the day.
I'm never stopping in the middle of a
season like this mostly all I miss... are any
reasons not to persist.

I'm on the stereo, lines that don't slow down. Remix so easy as time goes down.
Fashionable structure from my head down from a crown. Hyphenated apostrophes.
All around a sound. In the clouds. My chemistry, a ragga tip, the future's equipped, and loud.

In an essence, here's my presence, pressures make me jealous, why should I lie?
From life to death, I'll know I'm blessed
With lyrical reasons that pass any test.
In the past, I've acted fly, why exaggerate
When with a reality tie I'll never die.
Bleary ignorance has blown me here
It is nice, so easy to drop sense when I try.

Liberated, I'm proud, to science the passion

Talent from this man never fake as I extend my plan.
Figuring fulfilling creations, cause I give a damn
Huge is my foresight and narrowed the finest jam.
Educated through fiction, picking up on my diction
Definitive strategy serving me through years
Take a breath of what's near I'll make it possibly severe.
I'm not tiring, mixing up picking what is firing
Serving corrupt, and trying to stay on top of such abrupt.

Particles accelerate, faster through our minds, together on a wavelength can save a lot of time.
Be behind yourself when you want to relax, in front of your past when you're after the facts,
On top of the world in a new future, pact.

Taste my tact, wicked as I inform,
breaking down for reason in the track.
Wondering, consuming this dj's
coming back, hack,
I'll never be the last to attack an unjust
comment,
Justice, like ambiguous to my cause,
often my favourite case,
I'm not putting any holes in the wall,
but I had to tell you, explain it to you all.
You can do this, surprised and yes you
can see me.
Check my harm I'm only digitally
receiving check the code I know I'm
mastering,
Intelligent stereo-phonic pleasure
splendidly automatic
Animal to break the law of time and
alter space the future's a clause erratic
and here is the rest of it.

I met the new fate of a date with pure
taste not out to prove, just cruise the
case.

Just the same zest, I put my art to the
test and recognise I am fresh.
Never despised I'm just too wise for that
old fright night side
Get my act together and turn you
white, polite, I never bite
My mind on my duty, my mind is my
time. Surreal sidereal like a dream and
entwined melody
Disco ordinate no function in studio
concept
Accepting singularity since a new
advent I've still got my pride, dance
with the key.
Try to act like, try to talk like, try to be
like, the only one on the mic at this
height is me.
Creating through another night a
hardcore scene
Avoiding mystery a strong believer
myself
Don't feel betrayed I'm just a section of
stunts
Kept to protect enough cleaner hype

Complete like a tact onwards I've got to
make facts that are with the same track.
It ain't so hard I believe I've acquired
that industrial strength formula.
Like bond to know time hitting lights
with well regarded rhyme.
Your choice is what I need to get by.
An invisible voice some might say.
Can hold a direction through the very
fabric of it's way.
But I can't pretend, energy I've seen in a
day
Patterns in the path of my patterns
never end.
Love, life, hate, lust I wonder why.
You cannot trust me, I thought you'd
sussed me. But now to my surprise I
even worry for my style believing it was
wild myself a home-grown child
I sigh for denial relieving any title,
receiving for a vital wish or prayer
So I am here, bad as I go on. Never
hypocritical to rhythms isolated all from.
Future shines strong I never thought I'd
go wrong.

Beautiful crowds offer alternative structures in my song.
I try to keep the story quiet, I try to keep it neat,
But with the authority when I remember searching sweet.
Mechanical for beats halcyonic, seducing the movement is long.
Numbers in brackets, collecting a vibe from a habit like a plan for a tribe I'm a creature that's existing
Through a clever life deciding not deceiving and you can have it, I am releasing this force
And you could map it although rapid to the next thing, scene, automatic conversation
To the new routine played, it's just the latest suggestion. Since the big fast inclination.

Too young to want to pour your life away on the narrow lines I stay.
Getting it together every day.

See mostly I like to share I might have thought that you didn't care
But I'll never be unaware and now you understand I kick the flair.
Never backwards or slow, initiatingly intimate intimidatingly resourceful.
Show me the man who can surely underrate this
It's cosmic, I choose to receipt cause I'm better. I see the light
And I'll prove that it's right until the day that I die. Seriously working what is fly.

Liberated to tell you what I can see, not just trying to sell you tales as the force creates a key.
Carrying my mind we often wonder hallucinating into the power that is waiting.
Customising the life that emerges, reindulgent the power is urgent.
Craze, best to delete a phase for what is real and in faith. So our life has space for a new atomic race,

So we have life for what is nice but what is the fission?
Can you taste a collision remembering that first vital decision.

Why fly past when you can remember answers to your questions, no fake
I'm just polite to pass my point over to you to smoke like a joint.
Virtual dependency, harmonic insanity, no such inscriptions,
Based now on a version that life must have it's missions.
Industry, narrow misses, politicians.
Tonight, rolling the bandwagon so bright,
Clipped, metaphysical but tough, we're not tight deciding what is enough, only love is up above.
How it is, fools breed like thieves. Fuels, you achieve from, music misdemeanours.
Life is a tremendous blast, like, to Venus.
People passing in my mind floating, here I'm only quoting Don't follow me,

you should be voting. Armed, trouble starts in technical colour.

Bitches in a magazine just never beats me, microphone biting, you might say I'm frightening
But I stay with a flow which is strictly enlightening.
Stupid? A word-search I never did.
Vivid, the scene through the lid of my...
Preaching, you know that life is bleaching. On the score I'm already reaching.
Kissing, crazy, what records have I got?
No record player I just mix and I blot.

Blessed not just with a pen, back like a radio, I'm in control, it's any thought I know
And in the studio, analogue it's a vibe. Who's on my side?
Why I am blessed with the reason for rhyme, unquestioning time leads me to decide that

I could be licensed for my unofficial recital, big bites coherent but no bites from me.
My mind testing hard how a reality can free me, looking back I'm only steaming
Future intelligence, ideas and a dream leading our answers like fluid in a stream.
We've got to take care with this sense and hardcore
Although the message is clear you know what it's for... fair?
And now don't you think that I won't be there.

When my dj drops the rhythm it is a virtual vinyl collision as he makes a new decision
Wicked, matching up sound effects cutting up are fluid breaks.
Collecting mixing methods every night through week to week.
He can catch the animal and through the technics we speak.

Back and forwards the crossfader
tweaks into an atmosphere that won't
chill out so neat.

Reality bites, the original scratch, my dj
like a demon has the knowledge and
the knack.
Known to forage for the right track,
bassline creator with an exclusive pack.

So is it bad if I figure I'm gift within my
riff? I know my maths backwards why
deny I can lift
Any crowd as it happens, keep your
reckoning in effect when I'm back I'm
bad and bold as I wreck. Enough
checks before off to the final frontier on
the attack, knowledge has it's
boundaries no fear. My crew can care
just like the record deck still like the rope
chain round your neck.
Next forging new talent, stoned I create
and off into the sky
We're all in time with what it makes, so
clear as it is bad and can comply.

With our lyrical reason it's time to intensify.
Enormous what the beat is now releasing, teasing, my better style is pleasing.
Instant mechanisms, feeling great, memories that I make...
Passing the days, my mind like a maze cool individualism the format I create
Not so complicated now I'm thankful.
Concealed doors and protecting walls.
In this life we all possess there's nothing more, simple, an angle. Waging a war.
Like a portal I won't forget that I have equals who also
As we speak through mental quarters, tropical topics and how long I may take
Reasons have a virtue back breaking though I never mean to hurt you
My true blue I sing along in constant melody like my doctors remedy
I transcript the right so you can feel.
Done up tight just like I speak.
You know the language works every day of the week

63

Basic, it is just heaven I am under,
complicated incapable of blunder
Friends like lightening treat my enemies
like thunder.

III

Galaxy defended, universe and solar
system never ended
The size of some things leads me to say
I'm mended.
Blending with the next beat so far
going on , in , round
Around in a test I seem to say I'm proud
of now remembering the beast I am
down.
I know God understands in my hands
super-elements, supreme developments
Some candid idea with radical
evidence.

The reason I'm here achieving what is
justified
I just had to have mentioned, all the
time I am going to try.
Designed, it's for our culture future
sound for the future sound keep
moving.
Under our feet the ground is assuming.

With the information I may peddle,
settled, unqualified words for my
homes who afford
Back across the board, in for real, cause
my secret is a formula to conceal.
You know it's happy to be active, in the
squad you can catch this
Happy to be active, mean when you
relax it's...
Happy to be active, in the squad you
can catch this happy to be active.

Concept persuasion a modular
guarantee of where we're going with
symmetry

Hold the crew as I say what I afford I'm the boss of this secret world.
All active every note written like a teacher always rocking faster lines that scorch.
Down now you can only try, designed by me only true that it's fly.
Happy to be active, mean when you relax it's...
Happy to be active, happy to be active
Happy to be active, mean when you relax it's... happy to be active.
I've got to divulge you if it's a scratch that you're after, it's the states that I alter
Happy to be active, I wonder why the truth is so difficult to find?

This is very difficult to say without the proof.
I've been around, but now I'm growing up where is my youth?
When I'm outside on a corner I'll be wondering. Who's really winning, whose really with the truth.

From the time I started, no need to rough it. My thoughts are clear set apart from buzzing

I wonder who is, into peace, into war. We've got this far and now it's time to realise.

Paradise missed or did it leave a scar, my mind is like a missile, my body like a car.

Top of the range, just the flow of the trend back with the objects, making new friends.

This competition's just a gain game at ease with the elements, other rivals are driven insane.

With the constant mental pressure. You should recite and see your whole life fresher.

The scam is you are your own middle-man, you may not like it sometimes.

It's been a thought through decades and a plan. Take care of number one. Yourself, your favourite fan, the brother who succeeds indeed is a man.

Basic instinct, I catch the next link, down with a reason that won't make you think
Unless you have to, surpass clues. As quick as the front page from the everyday news.
Maybe I'm made, the way that I'm saying I've a remedy to any delaying
Choice from a full range to help you decide on the music that I'm playing.

Sure, in full effect what I can do, overlooking the principle that there's enough space for you
In the past I've left a path and you now know that it's true, no errors and
As I'm evolving from finer elements, do you remember?
Even at this pace the latest case from the sender.
Shine, I'm never going to waste a line. Intelligent input
A message from my mind just to make sure you're always high and dry.

The problems start if I need a picture to fit in my mind
Sometimes I might derange as estranged I will feel
Maybe to the photons, protons direct chemical
A lot can go on, round, down.
Always I like to write to music, with I know I now swear I'll never abuse it,
Can be so soothing though I watch my spelling, punctuation.
In, on through I stay observing.
Another burst and I aim to let it loose
My most positive try, I'm not learning to fly
Raver, learning to read, so that I can know. Bad drawn back like an arrow in a bow.
But like a poison what can I show? I'm over with ease if you've ever tried a drop
It's like a box, no threats, an equal in full effect of the deepest dread.
Of course I mix, ain't we all into the finest fix available in life.

However you may sow this is a feeling for your heart never easy.

Smear of light, wide and thin lines complete my sight.
Colour coded volumatic through the dark for any rough heart, sonic.
A chaos for modern day, same to say Love.
Understanding borders in reality from above the rhythm is corrective plutonic.
Shapes in the sky moronic, beats and bassline, on the set like a chronic
Fix to please you, elements you deserve mix that'll leave you gasping of thirst.

Warm like on today. I hear a storm in the summer sun of quality, like a laser gun!
It's like working 24 hours a day when I'm asleep I make up my pay
It's a big bad box each way I face, get out of my way I'm in demand I had to say.

I think I'd better unwind I've got a word for you and all your kind.
The game is wicked, I've just got to hear it on with the score like a fearless sniper in effect.
Synchronising, discerning and on the block swift
I've enough pride to see another excerpt cut by a quality emcee.
Sometimes so low I can't chase the bubble on my own
To start with is trust and device that I have known.
Strict my standing order, notes above my head collide
I'm not the only emcee who can take a ride this way.
Glossy, there ain't no time but into the function
As a sliding line, in the right direction is a sign to create like I mention.
I'm glad that you can notice my touch rapid like a rush

Back for a queue so longed for and never in the way. Owed to a flavour of rap fresh today.
As of course deep response in the league you might get shown once.
I run the risk of being sarcastic I drop a vibe and immense facts.
Looping old school tracks a hardcore mac's back
When I return the feeling's not drawn it's got the knack. Beyond comparison fall out my brother, sister mind the flack.
I'm a virus, my mind is blackened and black, dark
Balanced, alternative forces in my life create the spark cutting in not to bite
The future is forged through technology hype.
Human conditioning seen through the rap that I recite itself a strain to the modern living of life
Ripe I offer past time that is clear occasionally down my knowledge never in fear.

I guess that I'm acknowledged I try to adhere to extra special vibes and sounds that are all new

With my lyrics extensive, suggestive, line up and be calm, you won't have another quip.

Inexpensive reality to let you know how deep consciously collecting what should be a feature

Conclusive study designed by me still rolling like a creature, a major rave preacher.

Producing producer all the time finding a use doubling-up is my hardcore view, a decision

Digitally revealed a new incision, the master mission.

My soul is now visible to my eyes it feels so good, it is hard but I do not have to try

Incredible sculpture as my mind manifests if everything I want to be I'll find out what is best.

Into my reality I take a test, wait, taking plains testing checks, all for the realm, no prehistoric breaks.

I catch the frame leaving another time and space for my head

Why? Cause I'm down with past nostalgia and I'm the fastest and the best.

I guess I simply never told you, my life obviously fresh.

I always found that if I plan how I'm reciting

I can be frightening, intimidation on the mic I won't be sedating.

Aggressive through the night my dj highly rated and in Dolby in your home or car on cassette

We're aiming to make sure this mix you never will forget

I'm training as I touch the patterns, trailing flaunting a standard that I've never known to fail

Am I in demand? I wonder as we continue, a radical fairy tale land.

Essays that I'm testing are only fresh,
back to the beat, hardcore messages
Mystify as intense as you're feeling. Dry
when I'm in the public eye.
I must survive, others have been left
dreaming, no fault of mine
It was themselves they were deceiving.
I'm in control of a vital receiving.
Relating to intelligence that adjusts,
that's just like us...

I hope it's not just my decision to
change and accept
New-age power feelings, dramatic
dreams and reasons.
While in a fine-line God I have a trust.
Now check my bassline bump, we've
got enough.

After careful consideration I decide
how to feel I have enough time to
formulate this rhyme.

Cold, in prose my latest biographical
memory under rated, blatancy, radical
through new relations
Automatically concealed until it really
needed to be revealed.
Check my shrewd identity on the make
As I pass I see the fortunes that I take.
No mistake, I never front just smoke and
realise
That how we're living leaves no time for
dull bystanders in a line.
This is for my friends who never saw
me as a sign.
Tangling intellect yes I am so direct, so
connect
To this talent with the power of a jet.
Respect, less my dancehall ever forget.
I'm getting newer as my words become
a set, raw
Make you work your mind till it's sore,
take you to a new place.
Of latent dimensions to adore, injecting
feelings to the wise,
Naturally based through crucial hip
hop I intellectualise.

What is going on now, well did I have to ask? Problems left intensify burning in your past.
How it is and how you cope are important to the last, be patient and treat with kind in your path. Intricate heroism heralds as we laugh, complicated architecture compared to what is fast.

Indecisive elements are on the set smooth, looking forward to a time when we're all improved.
Feeling good I only figure what I may, back to back since yesterday
And on the groove I dare to train I'll never call final, cause I don't want to drain
Energy from a sense so fluid, I'm serious in this dream like a druid.
So no pain my mind is scoring big bonuses as I'm checking the same.
Why do I feel so worried by my future? Seen

And how I hurry from a past time green
into radical compartments.

Where contestants and competitions
are the roll in no war like conditions.
Honestly into knowledge that don't
dictate
I'm a high plains surfer staying away
but not from fate as I remember now
we can relate.
Heaven plus intuition lead me, for I
reckon as I need breathing through our
souls we'll be achieving
Looking back won't leave you meaning
neglect. Be positive advance with such
effect.

Immediately, eventually happy to be a
raver. Eventually beckoned by my lifestyle's behaviour
Back to face is a moral decision at my
command I'm in demand.
Fantasize, the real dice we control so
you see the dexterity of my mind

Slip with yours, play tricks I never bore
the best on the toys the one to run riot
Clear to your eyes when the vibe runs
deep I've got to joke through the
smoke to hit sanity
On the two turntables I'm a prophet, a
Pharisee on the two quartz lock vicious
divinity.

How many lines, times do I have to
roach to be my own boss, coach
Reckon effects in secluded interlude to
finalize my mood, it should be
understood
I'm a multi core raver with mathematics
to endorse my own front.

How many lines? How many rhymes,
names, faces, places, tracers, plans and
cases to still be
Able to face you with the bass I
construct is this home never running
out of luck?
Folding space and time like paper.

My life could be much better, trying to
suggest a moral way to spend my time
In and out of days in a number of ways
socialising congress on what I think
Before I have to blink.

Kicking' it to you unless you live abuser
If you keep your mind clear you won't
be one to loose, all of the factions that I
have are never crude.
Following a sense itself to discover
moving my mouth not like any other.
When I like to go off I go off like a
nutter, bread and butter, letters change,
rearrange
Just like this vital vinyl flutter. Virtual, I'm
too kind but I suffer redefining quality
atmosphere.
It's alright I can relate to the wicked
structure of reality created
I have a heart as I roll my thinkings into
territories unknown.

I'm rated, in an understanding mated to
this custom so sedated.

Back to match your questions as I light
I've got to wonder if it's fated, belated.
I'm at the top and I won't stop until I
have dictated.
Learn how to feel, I know that you will
as soon as you taste a serious attitude
somehow in the right Place, never
down, real time, working like an
interface,
mathematics from the quantum bass, a
link unto a finer place.
In the back of my head am I still
dreaming? Although through the
substance I believe in
Distances are crossed that were earlier
seeming indescribable, my eyes just
want to stare.

Weird, why my wisdom must care,
reality achieving time and space are
misdemeanant.
I'm left so I can reveal any necessary
form, shape, frequency, function always
fly

My mind a bomb, this emcee's life-style
versatile as I stand witness I start to feel
warm.
Lyrics through the microphone electrify,
intensify as I calm with my words.
Warn, I can only do justice touch this
and recognise a new dawn
Magic, an intellectual fission the raging
mission hard to the core, social effect.
The new feedback. At last in this land a
law. Coordinated precisely, based on
premises before
An intermediate spark coloured in the
dark vital, summarised and equal.

The new magnetic quarter, sustained
orchestral beauty
Holophonic, just like a force, natural
ability, balance.
Symmetrical advance no ghost of a
second chance digital symphony.
I base my findings into actual fact
feeling are laced through this rap but I
may act.

I won't let you forget I'm on the way back in an attack mode my vocal never slack.
Who is my rival, can you decipher? I'm no new writer on the definitive verbal track.
I am commissioned through the hype ahead of the pack
My tact I've packed information in condensed form, no gaps.
I aim to crack previous intentions with this grammatic weapon
Dimensions run true like waves on the sea all mystic procession, ascension follows me.
I shouldn't have treat you like that.
You're worth much more and I realise,
If I treat you like you don't care our relationship would fall and neither of us would be here.
Sometimes I just wish you'd slow down it makes me frown, I think that you don't understand
I should have explained it yet sometimes I've just learnt

Don't you know what I've found? My
soul races on , my feelings get burned.
I wish I could see you, it is nice to be
needed if I am I can be considerate, to
my life there is a plan
I used to feel it was wrong and I am
damned
But now with myself in the future I
practice teachings that are real.

Never too late to include a new deal,
surreal
Bilingual strategies part of the wheel,
my system
Hurtling complexities of speed through
which I see a course.
Never looking back since I started here
are my words.
Spectators listen to my language and
you know that I hope they rate this
Kinetic narrative understood like a force.
Next time I'll take a shot
After carefully examining how I look
and what I've got.

Since advice I have worked on,
amorous gravity left embarked from
The place that I trip from, electric
kingdom, an emcee with the right to
try.
My reasons like patchwork every
opportunity to redefine this destiny.
The quality of my audio, superior
suggestion,
Passing lurid questions figured in my
memory, I'm stopping.
Paths in my rhythms not forgiven bring
it into sight like maths arranged to be
quizzing.
Atmosphere intention you should
know that I'm up, I'm on a mission.

Thinking big the next decision I've been
listening to a collection.
That has forced into reason radical new
projection.
The incredible procedure a lesson not
another version of this

Are you living in the jungle mists? Catch up with the plot I will not leave you in the pits.

After enough fine text and magic I decide that one can handle this climate. It's hidden construction in function is grand as I open the invisible like a door with my hand.

Now I'm living on a frequency everything goes as planned I get out of performance no ride that is bland, at what cost this fantasy? Built for the day

Formulated for the way I'm talking a new percentage will leave you walking I've got to say since my coherence pays I take backhanders from digital decays.

I'm not a new persona just around for the rave my technique is what the old days crave.

Down I am in pursuit, in the control seat I'm made.

There's some compliance between any unknown territory and the hype I may shade

Frivolous any doubts I have and vital
are my plays in this game
When it's not quite over I can't leave
you the same.

I tell you the truth, this tune don't lie. I
tell you the truth, this tune it don't lie.
This tune won't die.
We're in for real, no concealing my
                              belief to
your appeal. The quality of tone a
                              pleasure
just to feel are you with me?
Some questions are answered
correct I like to try
and sort my work out with respect
Standard commercial hype I'm going to
write, what do you expect?
The heady virtual clearings I inspect.
I tell you the truth, this tune it don't lie,
won't die.
I tell you the truth, this tune manifest,
intensifies,
it's order of energy runs a rule across
                              the

skies... As dark as it gets. The finest
                    infusion
a fuel that I won't forget.
As I reindulge, my experience shows.
Electricity for your ears and your eyes
I want you to know! A language you
                    can
manage when my prose is too fly. This
                    tune
it won't die.
I may get fed up with the way I'm blue,
alternate scheme letting my friends see
that dreams are true.
If they ever dare my romance is
intelligence to share from the
beginning the chapter filled with flair.
Filed with care giving it up to Love and
devotion when they're there.
Crazy to believe any standard or
concept that ain't mine I try to
sophisticate my wickedest syndicate,
Bilingual bass is moving it dead into
time dread back on.
So like I state in this rhyme, total control
quartz lock. And I feel fine. For the

future so shocking I'm not into
mocking, explosive just like real life
we're talking.
Gadgets and info., tomorrow's data
and virtual intro. Slides from a video
make you want to see the sequel.
I'm never giving up at this vital stage,
untold story unfolds from a new page.
This instant reaction to my frequency
change, notes so illustrative range.
Coordination laser specific into your
mind, turning, speaking, unquestioning
the time
Crying consolidated moderately over
connected blame.
Problems any of my friends may have
upon the craze.
Distressed, like a battle's haze, when my
messages phase.
I'm not giving it up anymore for girls
who are dazed. Left unarranged are
the passings in a membrane. Automatic
as I localise the pain.

Hopefully concerned for if I make the trip again. One hour and a half away since realising insane.

Break the coaster on the grounds that aren't the same. I feel deserted, there is no gain. But why are the rules so similar in this game?

Virtually connected through a Love. As the clouds scrape by, infinity up above

My life is living high in the sky like a dove.

Crashing through the orders until I have thought of Enough.

Big as I bring my rapology down like a seal

Not an apology I have learned to live through what is real.

As I steal, sweet intent, my new effects are trait. Never getting faint here's what I state, in a feeling interesting reason.

I'm calm dispersing what is agile leaving what's priceless fragile.

The ten hundred metal effect drum kit, my

phenomenon is fly dedicated to the sky.
Devoted to Love and all reasons why.
                    Back I
envelope your forces that try,
Complicated underrated I am by.

Through written procedure merely
hardcore what I need.
Aim to fill you with tastes you
remember I can see. Only to cross the
new point here with thee. Nuclear
common by standard I hear and sense
the machine.
Back like a dream which rivals particular
so into the scene mind expiring
exploration.
Devoted articulate deck checking know
                    how,
existing future is apart from you now.
I just try to get a glimpse of your smile
realising I ghost I just forget as I release
for a while
Not knowing where you are can lead
me on as I try to slide.

I figure I could panic sometimes it's very cold. If I forget I know that I like to be told
In a dramatic way, in a sense an equation.
I rehearse everything for authentic publication.
Appreciation of my knowledge is well reserved. As designed this notation
Is carefully selected in my world.

You know what really happened? My life sort of blackened
Now I'm clean from a cause I was flat with
I correspond my not only act to fathom from a mediated plan while remaining active.

All these are for you everything that's here, anything I might have done
All the facts devoted to the new denoted and assumed. I admit that.

On accounts so positive it's emulating attitude focus in control I'm going to grip
That schedule as I'm auto cued, I owe to thoughts I knew.
You've doubted but as I'm placing not for doom
This is a game you can unscramble I'm never decoded too soon.

Glad to see so much emotion, well am I? It's only a question but I'm full like I can be
Amazed, through rules laid deep I storm on top of the hype always and I warn.

I've been gathering these abstract tips upon my mental life I'm crazy, I am rap. I consider fly
But why push? I know myself lucky to be born able to try. I know that this is warmth

I don't regret any second feeling from me I take the chance and play it once Strictly ruling, I'm not abusing. New figures order logic for the tenses we're all choosing.

On a winning streak I'm never loosing, back my bets you all know I'm improving.

My space is always ready for more words frequency multiplying as I touch down

There maybe security in this new clear sound, I'm staying renowned.

Crystal clear my method, idyllic construction, an audio function

In blue, how could I tempt with what's not true?

I've been breaking ground for so long now, not always good

I'm talking as I should and you would, I have a trust

Dimensions must, another rush and you're believing,

In what was seeming, it's my new lust

I'm not shallow but achieving I am in quality not here deceiving as she receives my releasing
My wondered spiritual destiny in the future coming pleasing.
I try to shorten any teasing.
But I don't want to get in your way, what can I say, I'm almost made
Finding the trace of a unique shade.
Sonic glade your mind creates an incredible feature of altered states
Stands intense, no late related action the stone cold function is a faction.
I've seen street fashion, a collection I'm getting by into gear why should I make you fear?
I felt lucky when I woke up today, now it is dark. Am I demoralising? I've got to start
Winding questions and reasons is smart overtaking my own mind from a force
Pulling apart, my motion is art I've got to let you know that I have a heart.

It would benefit me if I'm now placing at large. No argument is recognised as I'm playing how I'm racing.

This is the rhythm I want you to be tasting hardcore mixing up like a mirage.

Our Love's automatic surge I search through the course. So incidental like modern life. Original words.

I've been waiting for so long for someone to talk to me.

It's a shame when I'm just honesty with a beat I see a vision and I realise something neat but I need Love to make my dreams complete. If I miss you I just weep I wish I'd keep my head up from the deep. Am I specific? Last night another dream,

What must I need besides your heat?

IV

This is very complicated but I know you
relate formulated and stated I must
move on with the day
As I create. Loneliness has only ever
kept on with making me late
So I'm always clever as I focus on the
date
This latest release will never cease
making my mind work setting my body
into peace.
Pictures in my mind lead me to be
revealing, the feelings you've had
before are already believing.
Caught like a chemical, conceived,
composed, put together like the time
and the angles.
The places I suppose. Patterns in the
carpet like maps of the sea, lights in
your mind
Folding symmetry. Back with the cause
but no end to see. The force in our lives
fresher destiny

For the projects the future is our habits. Sometimes I've felt like the last raver on Earth I don't know what to do, I'm getting mad. Should I go on? I've got the nerve intimidated only by a struggle.
I find the collision but am amazed At such virtual discussion enough to leave you in a daze. My writings change I'm checking arrangements, ultra cause from ultimate creation Backing an acknowledgement of vital dictation in this notable viable freedom for how it goes down. Is your influence sound? Pieces and pieces make up the ground, a target, gravity, to me renowned.
Instruments to measure pure time and real the blood pumping in my veins. I've got my lines. Blatant method. When it started, it wasn't long ago, I had to learn quick. How to be a dj that wasn't like another cause I'm the fastest Leave most of my audience in the dream team cause I've passed it.

Like a fashion, so I know how long it can last so amazing to be dazed again in the so typical ways.
Notated so I know that I'm committed to strong songs and similar sense.

With my cool words I want to rap to deep heads, I know satire is my freedom
Knowledge and power deliver their pay sometimes I'm quiet the key is in what I say.

Over convincing? I need a link together virtuous, reality I think.
Living in Love today, there is no other way and for the future I hope and pray it's going to stay.
Intellect winding I'm sighted research until I'm right now and for nearly every night
Honestly correct and politically tight. My diction never trampled justice from any sample

Over and able to create, my weight I handle a declaration, heavy narration? I take a pause for breath then carry on through sedation.
With my jungle techno plot I'm keeping secrets wicked but needing to be released,
Revealed, you know my needs, writing in the future I seem to meet my belief.

I Love and I Love the sound of space all around me, thank God for the groove
Or you could get lost in this place, how I keep up myself a drum and bass case.
Making those bodies move mixing I trade. The baddest tempos I've been known to fade
I make the grade here, the blast of my structure composed it is the finest high fashion shade.
Never too rushed following purpose constructed mood programmed in a touch,
I practice much to satisfy contenders I push.

Keeping with my lines I know why I came, cause I don't make things the same
Displaying lyrical chains with melodies I achieve again.

When I forget to force my voice up through my neck and out of my head
Voices come to me in satin red, explosive architecture.

From the start of what I said, and it's to all I've known, people I've shown, new age in decent tone
Apparent like a monolith of stone.
Creative, versatile from the direction which has blown.
Standing start to a pace with reason as a zone bemused by styles flown, I have seen.
Lyrically calm the insider of a dream to actually capture the emotion is my scheme.

At speed, no cost to me my competitors
must feel
On what I'm reading stating any
questions now of need.

Desire observed as a function lacking
no actual piece mixing up I mention,
dance floors I please
Conscious I follow leads behind me my
mortal deeds in my future the news of
the seeds I've sown
Stronger intensions from their growth
all alone until their flowering the altered
days just moan.
No difficult rules here through editable
knowledge that I loan.
When I am in front with sixth sense it is
design, refreshes my mind time after
time never blind
Into chosen secrets, whir gears and
grind truly innovative structures in your
soul it's plain to find
There I remind a logic underlined,
entertained the pattern I have framed.

Neither to release or contain any shame only the fine here is given air time
Hardcore repertoire from me more than a game into surreal fame and what's making it all mine
Tastefully matured like a wine slight like an incident forgotten this adds to similar rhyme
Happening creative like my every last line, energy is no curse and my ending always shine.
Realistic for your attitude as if I'm lying to be spoken as your envoy I'll be trying suddenly complying.
Truthfully taking from you inside information, narrative formulation. Adjectives sliced.
There's something wrong with my plan if I just need a hand it's only true, I like it loud,
Now it is down. Before you came things weren't the same. Now I am proud.

How can I play when you're not around? To feel the sound of the music that we make.

Reasons I take. Basslines that quake. Under my faultless minds that I break Energy moves in shadow less clues, currents not negative harmonizingly move

Seducing flow like a lake. Intimate initially reality my stake. Directive talent Not forgetting what I've meant dissolving I've digested most of the best. Behind the beat mixed up is nothing less.

I'm known to fly not hesitate as I make it through my lines.

Keeping my mind together since I've rehearsed for time.

Always on top with a new vibe never looking back since I began,

If I ever underestimate your ears, you know I've tried. With a sun blessed style that's bleached white I've learnt to keep a lesson tight, same versions. Usually different every night, my mixing's polite.

Rapping like this is good for everybody's sight.
You're not in my way, just taking it right
I'll never be out of any jungle techno hype,
My mind is like a scanner, the force is just a light, Behind me through confusion I'm fixing as I might. All the memories in this scheme set up, scheduled like a dream.
So realistic, this is the game onwards forever knowing what is clean.
Learning what's supreme. Initiative leads us to control the inner sanctuary beyond what is known,
Style thrown down like a reprimand appearing as you need, operational
Besides a unique post suggestion, vocational accredited to the mood as mentioned.
Still just as radical it's sectioned, when I take a breath just long enough to reckon.
You have got to let me know how you want it to be

We should live our lives together with our Love travelling free.
I follow you, you follow me, I need every beat that sets sincerity.
As I get to know you I'm liking what I see my last decision was to show you all I mean
A high altitude vision, a synaptic run so missionary naturally like us on collision.
I've got to take my chance when I can, independently on an appropriate frequency, immediately.
Music always has a message just don't understand it wrong. I'm going to say anything I may. These are the lyrics to my song. Yesterday you mentioned it less. Today I'm back with words I confess.
I always know! I have some friends I can trust for so long. I don't think I'm always changing I know the pressure drops when there's rhythms arranging Again my only rage a pattern corrected the next format every serious reaction.

Through my intention, sense through sweet detection.

To correspond with actual physical I let you know I'm over miracles

Deep in the force that's deciphered periodically renewed reviewed after the meaning's understood.

Measured and sectioned, I run this adventure like a true speaker, I'm no weaker

About to begin matters like teaching I'm keeping. Angels are sleeping and counted are cursed.

If I rap then maybe I have the chance considering Love, I know that I advance Face through time, I thought that it was life that brought us all together but it in fact seems never. So small because a craze is taught, follow pyrotechnics if you see that your face fits at all

With your whole feeling in it dare you ever consider your life force getting dimmer

The blow never dated as quick as we create it. I'm getting thinner, news essential.
Accredited at cost maybe no real loss. Laying down a new mental, as a flash, but who knows?
How to create light and put it into rows. I'm feeling the pros, I'm feeling the cons
No constrictions when I'm hanging on a long convenient conversation context continually
I conscribe to end eventually.
I don't want to stop, I pause for a breath and remember the lot.
It's not a catch I have to watch. Do I deal with the devil or deal with God.
I maintain my cause is so crystal clear with nothing to change that
The sky's the limit, the limit is the sky! Every time I see the clouds they make me wonder why
I recall the time itself seemed to stop in my mind

I realise the desire, hear the sign and know that it's mine
From the Earth and the atmosphere we're used to.
Sat behind my eyes I see a million colours waiting for a better time with my brothers
Basslines don't waste time roots through my energy repeated.
Reckon in effect when I rock I'm needed.
Coefficient equation forget it is the nature sent to your mind to let the data venture.
In the technique the proof you're never beyond moments in time leave me into the groove.
Ambient to put the lights on enlarged, my outlook in life, I am selector.
Energy from a feeling the way I can drop the speech sometimes as if it had never happened. A natural corrector spacing eternal directions.
Beware as for what I expose this runs true for how I decide inside my life.

You've got to know now as I've thought twice I'm bringing to you deeper feelings from the spice.
Coming correct for those that are worthwhile, never waste, this although it's fast profile
My faded assuming line, why is it nice? In your life you might have noticed a buzz
It can come from the music but there's never enough.
This is a warning, on the mic we're storming I've got to practice this habit is reforming.
For us all is a pressure through our moving, is discovering second balance only soothing?
Together is our space, no need to race, I am improving. Love my real Love and reality is grooving.
Back into the force as my mind's part of the tuning
Timing devoted my friend like an instrument and it's trace I am young as my past is often evident.

Here is my newest case, I plead dope, I'm always relevant.
Now I sit and reckon deep to finer feelings I can keep.
Beyond a threshold flesh is weak but you're unequal.
Not unusual like a freak fundamental incidental beyond the code so instrumental.
Accidental portrayer through manners as a loop looking deep I will find chemical hope.
As if you ever need this hype I deliver the clearest dope, ready wrote.
Deviously written as I decide every note. Hardcore, I'll never work it out Automatic as my sights have such aims I fly a fire through fame it isn't a game.

If I think from the beginning who is winning? Links and the arrangement is quizzing.
Final virtuality based now through infinity cool as ice in reality some divinity.

My commonest prose may induce a
flyer section no correction I'm speaking
casual suggestion
I toast this and mention. Sometimes I
know that I've never been away,
Although I'm into crazy scenes that cut
my day back up with no negatives to
capture.
Closer is the rave that I can say. If all the
people that I reach I can warn.
New dawn, fulfilment of all magic like a
storm and it's translucent boundaries.
Sets a state for how you found me
disengaged I'm burning on a solid fuel.
Giving you no new routines with any
reason I confuse.
It's in the clues, back to basics I am not
ever going to loose. Some things are
perfect like my rap and it's attainment.
Videola style construction as my soul's
no late survivor,
Rumoured to psyche out, psychedelic
revival through psycho tropic
protection

Cyberspace, I understand what I state.
Rewind the tape again and check out
my fate
I Love, stay with the one I date, info
through my outro is engaging so relate.
Controlled I figure life and it's
arrangement I'm tuned into the force
and it's behaviour
Through natural sources the other side
I might have met since our creation, so
plausible to show
Positive recreation like a radio active
glow. I hope that you remember this, it
ain't
Carved from stone, I admit the lifts
although I'm all alone. I stop the rain, it's
another cool night. I decided that I'll go
outside now and find what's right. How
I wish it was out of sight. No matter I
make my lyrics and I'm still polite. Fly
with the same nature as bright. I never
lie.
What can I say is it only today that leads
me to enough words in an unconfused
way.

Battling on, settling selling the score for other worlds, staying with the force
Focus, what I mean isn't hokus pokus, my wicked dj can jam, in a life of perfection.
Protection no rejection, function, my dj's collection, my last recollection.
A rave's perception, my friends intention a laser, so bright and after all
Just fulfilling my call, will I get through it? Even with my technique there's something I seek.
Street dreams and that's how it seems, as soon as I get to writing I know I'm learning.
.
So selling out, wide, believe me, no need to hide, what I like is the right
To be all, the fact I'm small, I never realised till it took a book to convince me
Now I'm back like a prince so where's the real crunch? Crowned!

Like all music analogue and digital the pieces control senses with their sound. Format for time, cool a line, camouflage less predictable

Hesitate for what you really rate, just a joke or met your fate.

I'm blessed with a word hold the crew as I say what I afford across the board in for real

I'm the boss, no secret scenario here's the formula. When you're in life you want to rave.

Checking out the stories every day in the squad you can catch this, happy to be active

Mean when you relax it's...

Next my party lines forget. I can never handle fresh, I need a secret melody I wrote.

Analogue every note placed as a teacher always rocking faster, lines that scorch.

If it's scratch you're after keep it unique, it's the states that I alter. Got to divulge you

It's merely the secret life of the other side. Down but you know I can try Designed by me specifically fly. I wonder why the truth is difficult to divide.

Whenever I may lift my voice to say a line that's correctively talent.

I leave behind a diagram of trying that's latent buzzing is just for the few so we're here in the present be patient, I'll lead us on up to another vocation with an urge I consider meditation

As many unlit corridors are starving for narration. Explanation. No degradation.

Life time guarantee a final declaration within sanity how fine and fly this one wicked emcee.

Sometimes my tongue is never wrong so I vow to syndicate inspirational song Cut creative special keys come along bouncing with the formula. Upfront be part as we party away. Dedication, that's just weapons I play.

Misinterpretation is nothing that I say.

Condemnation? I don't know, should I stay? Forgive myself like I did yesterday, I have a plan. Together we can, on my own life's like quick sand. Everything's sinking in, in hope you understand.
Records have an A side and a B set on a schedule that will make the party Happy is the note that reserves it's vote moving is my cousin that listens to my quote.
Positive hardcore the force behind our time quickening adjectives enhancing every line.
Tribal pure selection, wicked what we find. Jump on board our decks you won't need another ride.
Cool, considerate all is in our lives to believe.
On top of the world I won't run out of words till I bleed.
I figure the motion again and leave you to read. Crazy creation on the mic I supersede.

Designed to be faster my imagination I feed whilst colliding deciding reaffirming my side.
Taking it seriously cause there's no place to hide. Together my fortress, certain beats are new
Miracles on the dance floor, miraculous hardcore. New age not redundant.
But in the later years a natural awareness for your ears, a new course for your cares.
Just another burning jungle techno, yes a void, my power coming to you with a choice, specific views.
No further enemies as I deliver the latest news, never confused
Not often as I can be, I'll be paying my dues
In a rhapsody called content with a president that it's Heaven sent.
Together my words in a cool sense never a curse, cruel, in your eyes am I forgiven? In this mighty headstrong life I'm awaiting a collision. In this mighty headstrong life.

A new religion, the first incision, a surgeon's decision cuts close to the rhythm.

In my charms I'm lucky that I have speed, deliver you the message for which intensity bleeds.

I'll never fail on that step for a feeling that we need, like pleased I don't forget.

As I learn quick to believe my lyrics as quick as you read.

See, I listen to the lyrics, try to deny my gift but it has stuck, I recognise every riff.

Do you really think it's plain to see, easy to understand? I feel someone watching me

It's you with your heart and hand. Next time that I dream, I'll dream of you, and I can.

The path that I recognise, my soul which has been guided.

Leads me to secrets which lead me to wilder thoughts and desires higher than and higher.

My sequel, for calm, I only deliver sense, why break it off when we are intense?

Messages like notes, singers to unquote, passages and plains are here, only the buoyant float.
At first I thought it was just a part of life I can get it together and sounding nice It's now that I realise although in the past I've been ripe, I want to stay on top psychic to that hype.

You can make me, I never forgot, the music an antidote it's built into my soul My mind, so my body can be sincere, turning I roll. Turning I decide I know, but changing nothing, records in a row.

Wicked is the air that my set breathes, new automatic lip sync.
Although my hip hop will make you think it's faithful link,
Lasting is out to create such ever long breaks. Love like a behaviour needs it's takes.

Original requiem from no new
hardcore emcee following educated
recipe I'm checking the beat is
Intimidating. Sketched out like a skyline
only scribbled near as could ever be
from a future entity
From time travelling prodigy unique I'm
the master pilot since I've driven
through as I speak
Noise can record. Just sweet to hear
the session bleep..
In the mix there's no standard that is
going to leak. True I suppose, my style's
never weak
Yesterday was hardcore this must go
on for a while as I refine.
Every positive rap line for you to know
it's mine when I'm eventually happy
that everything's fine,
Eternally correct straight from a feeling
miles high losing no urgency is the
energy to try.
Whenever you're ready, I'm steady,
what worries me is I'm not like

everybody else. Words in my eyes intensify

Levels I endure like certain powers I feel endowed

So forwards is how I'm going to train other rappers in the game

Towards you my force is bowed strictly there to entertain.

Eventual cosmetology from me should start no pain.

Various industrial lines from me not quite the same eternally designed by my soul when it's insane

Near any remixing bordering lines the way I came, when rioting versions pave the way.

Every record I drop always has something to say.

Latest, back to old school are the anthems I can play

Four, to the floor with no delay, and again anything that I might miss now

Revolves around my brain jamming other signals ends my session from the name.

So any sound professor cannot duplicate, what I produce I never bite.

Now that we're talking a language you shouldn't over rate we've got to be listening.

To one another, other brothers try profiling style always makes me smile.

Once left behind but now I want to roll I ride with this crew when there's nothing left to do.

I'm living for the skies bust a disguise knowing what I know, learning what's wise.

Hip hop for my soul only raving for the eyes didn't mean to startle on the lines.

I take my time so you're digesting what is fine don't want to get too mad on the fluorescent pad.

Respecting what is mine introducing newer bad I was a fool for ever looking up to sin
Since the last fad, tradition I can begin drop the paranoia I'm sometimes in.
Like a fabled story does the gentle ever win? It's in the crystal for the transmission in the wind.
It's in the pressure of the diamond in the ring when I go to Heaven I hope they give me wings and make me sing.

Sophistication leads me now I am just so pleased reasons to get equal in the trends I believe.
Lyrically content, I have a trust in the speed I can achieve, directly as I need, finer forces.
Through moral choices when I see dedication leading virtually after present tense
All what's left is will be. A patterned texture just seemed to vex you
Through infinity, I'm still what I mean it's always measured.

And upto spec. this high tech step up is
rough enough as sectioned.
Almost nothing else to mention until
the time we need adventure.
Zoom into dimension, I'll be passing
keys independently as any final unity.
Cause you've got to take your turn to
find out electrical what we're about.

V

Life is instant and so clever I can vouch
in and out of consciousness as the
other side we touch
Energies push my favourite feeling in
my mouth. Next my mind always freshly
inclined
To know what's up. Such a direct
method now in bout.

I find with interest no fault my next text delivered graphically as requested
Similar lines from this creative emcee's mind will lead through harmony narrated
True experience my life a test-tube on display, scheduled not tasteless
Yesterday's hang-ups are sometimes tomorrow's new entities.
Relationships irresistible in my mind superior In quantities I'm granted with this quality
Inferno separated like the sun. A bomb of individuality. True since the beginning of time all my data, every sign becoming nature. Safe acceleration like you notice from adventure then solidity
Years beyond any doubtful reckoners philosophy.
Such beauty the eye can etch on this borderless terrain, it's the same
Entertaining factors I'm preaching never plain forever my chance is to multiply

Explicit infinity expensive hyperactive past insane.

Original fate I redefine what must avert you, next are extensive reasons in a virtue,

Like a merger a way our God will not desert you, energy reflected here accepted not excessive.

Superlative thinking in a world reported never negative.

I finish every day like I just want to say I don't live in the past,

My memory's fast, exotic, for feelings that last. Caught in a glance.

And adding tonic, my mixing's melodic and on it.

Believing in truth all my tradings are proof as I'm from it.

No fiction this borderline an unknown comet

In which intentions are seismic, projected, unconnected.

Reinterpreted for the moral subject selected. Be part of your ambition don't regret it.

Gather pressure when a motionless direction is clever.
On top of the divide and choosing the light we all decide,
Around my paths appearing indexed I high-light the ride.
Circling instinct realisation since untold reinvented through this passion outlined bold.
No occasional fault through my design that is on show so constructed by method on a low.

Headstrong notes of a mission, decisions, alternative permission
Passions and actions that I can't leave in a flash you've been listening
To this radical narration from an emcee in the past. I'm so fast.
Lately I've been very concerned for how my soul might act.
Some versions a crack, sinister pollutant's a fact. My revenge is back, a message of auto-attack black.

I know that my problems begin if I think I'm going to sin.
I want to win on the narrow lines I'm virtuous I have to sting
A fine concept, that I kept with, my mind a new sign
I've been behind better blind times, now I forward and rewind.
It is just passing the latest unique of such inquisitive asking.
Leaves me cutting the cost straight through a fantasy. Infinitely inevitably and anyway as stated
I am fated by my forefathers to be together, forever under rated.
Like a trap baited, since studying electric educated and graduated.

Right, so at least now it's decipherable, I thought it would be memorable but what overheads do I need control of?
Through a soul, a light only visible at all, the glimpse of feeling.

Factioned, bypassed fashionable my heart mentioned honestly the less I'm alone.
What I take on board is all that I start for energy needs a fuel, elemental law.
Now that I'm known you've seen what was before.

That we're all aware together, forces of nature so clever,
I am in no demise forever, my knowledge a saviour. Translated versions visible through my behaviour.
Now that I trust Love I will be able to coincide what I thought would never.
Magnetic how I aim to please fresh patterns are released.
I'm quick as my feelings from the belly of this beast.
Finishing like I know I can, I'm in demand, possibly fortune's easy for me to understand
Vigorous ability only proved through how I've planned.

It's a wonder how I can but through my practice I am grand.
Assertive, my friends, the measuring of conscience revealed automatic harmony in existence.
Collector of disintegrating images and frequencies through speakers,
Connected like a circuit and in turn to every single amplifier burning.
Chosen turnings earning force with each encounter applying burning,
This nature, no doubt that I venture any facing related, it's spacing.
My digital tracings so placed as I need never wish again, opposite tastings.
Leaving final virtual cases intimately sane immediately initial,
Eclectic from a single aim at a test settling what is best, this reality issue.
Always fresh, united over less definitely not protesting and next
Replacing tense performing on set letting thoughts forget. Every second I reflect.

Several new places that protect within a view automatically reviewed upon request.
When I first started I knew it was unique, such fast movement impossible to speak
Total self involvement for knowledge I will seek and taking territories redesigned to keep
My feelings in tune, like the crystal to the air, any meanings undone only answered by a snare.

Up to the skies I stare as instant and necessary as gravity I consider my plot and recite the whole lot.
For explanation my purposes are dropped never artificial in this universe of God
Related physics state that my truth is like a fire. Never muted, no secret desire.

This consulted equation runs from me down to you, it is suggested that barriers are waiting to move

So I'll improve. My Love is really there without a choice because of my voice. And any mind will never compromise or ever have to think twice here is the rule
Automatically frozen like my heart, I never bite. Sympathetically noise.
I'm getting back, now I realise when I'm nice I check I'm kind
Routine surprise happy in a headstrong way and wise.

I want to win, it's not a thing if you don't want to take part.
We decide and decipher as an art form through a motion.
Electric, maybe I'm addicted to writing it has been hyping.
A solution, new intention if I remember I can sing.

Fateful intention faithful what I bring. Serrated exchanging separating the links

Together in arrangement, mathematics that think. Coordinated sighting beyond any brink.

Ideas hit me when I meet my friends, I could relay a list of such automatic proportions then
Together with a notebook and a pen devoted are my notions wicked I am again.
Revealing gestures settling pressure for a lifestyle mental here's some pleasure
Now everybody's thinking since speaking time that unfolds into a place that is known,
The conception never slightly exposed, over recognised a condition rolls
As I convince pre meditating risks, links set the limit reviewed,
Repeating, resumed it has been beating coordinated subjects in a view, you know I knew.
Straight on course is my techno rendered blue I'm over and I'm tripping it to you.

Purposefully compiled to shock no keys to this lock as hard in my mind as a rock.
Beautifully ended my patterns, like a document amended convincing as a clock,
With a check I've a reason that can never be knocked, I'm schooling and leaving.
Tutoring, teaching and pleasing keeping all my radicals around that are believing.
Achieving similar practices I'm preaching further into your subconscious I'm reaching
Anonymous regular the messages from this caller multi singular I'm bringing
Convincing sophisticated metaphors hardcore finally releasing.
Just as fast with the letters that I'm breathing we're seeming,
United considerate and ultimately beaming never conceding.

Japanese some of my tactics like sign
reading, higher motives my purposes
are leading.
Chemical clicks, diagnostic kicks
enforcing energies so strong
throughout the mix.
I'm teaching you my flashback though
you know I'll never prove
Out to exist within my life I move my
limitation upon the raw tempo soothes.
Working as hard as one of my many
moods I'm just a servant to the plastic
I'm choosing
Clever my portrayal of rap nature clever.
Always amusing. To the virtual
interpreter including
Forces that I feel would ever loose me
so I battle hard as rivals confuse me.
A typical particular arrangement set
loose leave until I'm happy there's a
pattern of belief.
Like a machine, multiple functions
included besides this myself, family
seductive secretive and exclusive.

Air just like the talking I'm displaying has been lying on top of truth, revenge or any discussion,
Since suspension, suspicion, my adoption is as critical taken back, driven from the days of hip hop...
A mild scratch, renegade mind in control of the attack. The future's back!
Same senses measure up as they equal in pace in the heat of the race I co-ordinately place
Lyrical tangents with steadying bass until the daylight so narrow divides every state.
Nightly intervals, remixing until late.
Always listening to the music with the jungle techno taste
So rearranged itself a forecast case intermediately honest, abstract for when a battle is in haze.
I'm going to rave, substantial any phase within haste as if faster than light from an original face.

Ultimate as always in succession is my noise sustained throughout it's reasons in a choice.
People on my side in a version now together ever bright let's do what's right.

What we only prove, reasons not abused, behind and through the lines, Mystic prose only fed up with what? Nothing can bring me down.
The latest set, no regret, higher times. Nobody frown.
When I raise my trigger finger all the hip hop's on the ground in full effect. Good intentions, viable, I smile for a while, down I'm concise. No denial. Why don't I give up? My life's an X-file, versatile.
In fact I find immediate purposes laid before me tactile.
I'm talking of the talent my tale don't hesitate to understand,
Wrong now distinguished as it can be metaphysically from

Any element planned, interesting my dj talking never bland.
You're fly now my homes, matrimonies, anticipation of bystanders glancing at a beat.
If I ever think once I think twice just of what's sweet. Defensive are my kind.

As sharp as our feet, routine new advice from the heavens if you seek Closer still to speak through a dimension saved from boundless tension in a heat.
Since the end a new beginning has evented so centred, concentrated actual fact
Remember dimensions in order referring reality takes a new border.

Establishing strength re arranging in thoughts as unique is how I'm able to speak.
No lazy domination in the nature that I keep, forces I equip

I will not ever slip, it is in the valley of control I am so quick.

Discover the outrageous boundary beyond common knowledge as we know

Premeditated mix of a blast that will blow, designated as a feature, put together so,

This revolution has all the feeling I can show towards a freedom we're needing,

Leading I'm leaving the guaranteed maximum I can pick and still succeeding.

Lines here so light they'll never be conceding, are you believing?

Sometimes I'm scared beyond a radical theory stoned I smile

Bleary eyed every morning I decide and then just kick it for a while.

Energy revealed in my style, I was chilling in the UK when I had to say

I'm on the dial, I have survived through mental ordeals and trials...

Getting it together as I put my pen to paper, the ten hundred effect drum kit is a computer
And I'm a disciple, I've often tried, to my delight like a sniper, I thank God.

For the right, I am able, reconnecting all things stable, wicked how I speed
Up the pace of a fable. It is not too high a price, suitable and in a degree nice
When I wonder how it mutes, any pollution in the air is always sliced,
Catching up in stereo, twice mashing up macabre virtual vice.
Any alternative schemes for functions can be scattered like rice, again simple
This warning like a dimple on the fairy of religion's face, after all a place.
Probably beautiful, far, another well removed state, come to Earth just to contemplate our fate
Higher emotions and intentions are my case.
Finally I can wait, since considering this fate of late, my next date.

Another superior reason to relate. With our Love that is stronger than any hate. With a passion so complete I contemplate the together state.
Re arranged, negative reasons disengage and pass away.
Exactly conditioned for any day when I might say what is not grey
Conversely my method exceeding how I am paid, radical a past that is in shade
Evidence right here now shows that I'm made.
And anyway all this real emotion I trade is the greatest
The time I take always equal to the fade of a future grade,
I instigate ambition and serve up like a meal on a plate.
Over time investigating hidden rumours that are made.

My life is full of metaphors, rumours, superstitions, and abrupt inclinations of Love.

Know that I stay ahead of all my healthy
ambitions, my real intention a touch,
As I'm looking at as much as my head
could ever hold. Another rush, I must
have told you
Never will my versions run out, I am so
bold, concise super relations
Automatically and conversely cold,
magically arranged for future reasons
from the flow.
Such a long time in this world so true.
My collaboration positively new.
Men can hold a view, whether you take
or leave the force is up to you.
When and if you don't know what to
do just ride upon this interlude.
A second interview reveals my
prospecting groove just to be a view.

No bad news here as the wickedest
mention has broken through.
So when I read a vibe it's always good
advice for my life,
That I should focus from, interrogate as
our passings enter fate.

Long solved equations of the never state relate again,
Justify the plate. Only confused by empty actions not my fashion. Settle my emotions under passion
Left on a plain, sliding entwining divine electric and on time.
It is what I say that I've got to watch as the plot evolves
Controlling elements eliminating sound and enticing profound. To me a lot has gone down, renowned. Expansion is knowledge,
Decent sophistication my safest bet, always honest.
As long as I'm in the life I live, I have a face to give, images impressive, my technique,
You know will never let me down, lower values are covered, I have to introduce initial cares,
Vital as said my music a new sound, particular checks through no obvious ground

Moving on a journey coincidental since found, automatic, adjusted and styled with flair.

It's back! Once they said that it couldn't be done, it's here!

Eventually I'm over forgotten yesterdays, they're near, do you like how I say?

Influential is what matters and a sanity will stay forever in a loop

Not about to decay when there's too much hope I've got to scope.

This hip hop here prefers to rave, listen to my answers in a stage

Why deny effects electric, I can save in grammatical haste.

Watch this space, total trance is period my case. As I settle obscure minds with a taste of my bass.

The newest selection of radical breaks can you intake?

Still the finest what I multiply and never a mistake.

I just lead with subsonic quakes for me
easy to make. While we remix and
match the complicated to a fate.
I control the rapture, from the forces in
my mind.
Previous feeling lead the want and find
I've accessed.
Love, Elysium, sympathetically I
captivate some of what they want,
meanings from above.
Ecstatic coincidence means I double up
and rush enough
Confused only by the smallest forms
abrupt. Locked lyrically.
So plush, never looking back on a class,
it's not my way.
Now that I'm here to stay, individualism
is the only worth.
Don't be lonely in your beautiful life on
Earth.
Re indulge, it's always fresh or would I
say
Pleased as fascinated, entertaining
every day,

Sensuous conceptions satisfied is all we wish for
Relief of bliss, related extensions may exist.

A selection of clear vibes amidst the jungle sound, resolution loud.
As transparent as proud, like high Love smashed never seen to suffer
Panoramic itself not like another, the clouds might seem to utter
Their cycle ascertained, no doubt infallible as cover.

Master of explicit director of graphical needs in words.
Please suspect or recognise a higher sign or escape from my tactic
Made to explore, emancipation like a remembered lover,
Unfetter, better a release so free obtaining a new natural key.

My mind clear, minimal expression is near, a laser not intimidating although

usually severe can pierce the
background alternating tastes of sound
at any altitude, remuneration of the
ground, superficial
Taking the test then just so proud,
initially to not be missing almost
fragrant lines I am listing.
Always insisting, alternative schedule
here to visit
Co-ordinately placed till every face like
no finer case.
Kinetic mischief from my virtual instinct
over morals, resistance how we think.
Beside releasing audio pressure
something sometimes quick
 Versus the beat, a reasoning frequency
shift.
I don't get this, you know that I am
equipped with a tongue that can get
me through the thin
And the thick, but I'm sick.
A few weeks ago when I was lonely I
realised everybody around me just
doesn't know.

Now I try and keep together that with which I was always clever but now never

Arguments occur every time, protection or interference it is not clear. Just why endeavour?

Are you really near? Or am I severed? I'm living tethered seen to the end of time so well weathered.

I'm sorry if my mind sometimes escapes me it's my method.

I'm a new man now as I hype how I'm going to write, recite chemically polite.

I want to be what I want how ever is necessary, cool but tight.

Redefining a fresh light, hypnotic high good for lovers insight anytime,

I've just got to splash for rhyme, never indecent one of a kind.

Call it a virtue, so fine. I often mean to tempt with every line.

Running forever true is this sound from a guru, not abrupt, I always felt like I knew you.

Through the signs, amassing state, relating index on the make

So strong is the creator that sonics will quake.

Realising I'm reasoning another version you can take. Words I can figure fast never fake, I'll never give up, passion what I break.

My mind doubles this flow, I had to tell you, this'll sell.

Miracles captured for opponents to believe, I stop and watch an ocean breathe.

A serious role considered, I don't have to bleed, showing well.

If I was logically infinite I'd get down cause you know I'm just missing it.

Never confusing it, digital, always choosing it

Ballistic, yes all collection I mirror, some suggesting reflections.

I've got skills that sometimes won't chill Feelings that I know are ill. New understandings I have made

Developing traditional fades so that you can get close
As I am to the noise, a superior adjustment in this, still tangling with the ghosts.
Succeed at your choice no narrow individual elements in my voice.
Releasing the most of which I thought was able, any day on pitch or delay.
The devious magnetic quarter, devilish mission complete.

I watch the clouds in Heaven and never cry, never weep.
How much automatic right now in lip sync set free
From so many patterns I keep, don't follow me like sheep.
I have right here what you might seek.
I can think now if this world is just re arranged on another plain.
Would you be someone else or in more or less pain?

Have a different lifestyle, face and name? It is the same until you want to notice

How some people never is a shame to me life told this. In my game I can give all the advice

Related to what we want to do right how you perceive everything that's around you justified is as you like. Love not as scarce as gold dust

Find what moves you if you must, true identity reveals pleasure beyond your lust.

Shaking competitors I have seen what do they trust?

Independence my deliberate machine is how accidental I crush

Together is my force through a dream I know this much.

The energy I receive back from the flow is something, radio one keep it alive and jumping.

They take my rhymes, I'm not surprised I settle myself equal, it's just a vibe that's always pumping.
Can you assume or imagine the jungle in the making?
Forever in time and styles that we're wanting, raving.
Dedicated decisively nice is how I'm staking
I never ever let the needle in the groove go into skating.
Bumping, chasing what figures swiftly like a kiss for the tasting
Relating, educated what we're facing.
Dramatic although my every intention a question.
So in my dreams it happens, everything that I want as at night like a laser.
Hoping clear cause my moving is sincere and in the right places
Now I'm nearer since sonic races and explorations I've been grading.
Crazy specific conditional routines forever shading, it's a sin.

153

Right here how I begin and exactly
within a tone, fulfilling a scene
Is how I'm living, we're in control of this
thing, like a motion, let it roll.
This is a story about living life slow, it
should not be your intention
When there's a score that you should
know, safe as I mention.
Finding new protection blowing so
For the direction, dedicated low,
supposing we go,
This is the best that I can show as for a
time I have to wonder if you were ever
going to say no.
In a ride there have to be conditions,
agreements.
Between you and me so we're seeing
what is seemingly revealed,
Every new concept conditioned free
you're always re entitled to be with me
Here and now, each other's heroes
from a history confident like a ministry
flying in the beat
Completely wild the way that we
exchange heat.

I'm wondering if heaven's got a ghetto.
Records are my point.
My stereo is high but I always do
remember the joint,
It's acceptable brilliance, JVC or Hitachi,
Technics or Sony
If I'm in the game at all it's because of
the way women re zone me.
My mind a new scratch every other
second all I see is the Earth leap.
So I've got to keep into my maxing style
that's not too creepy.
Most of my release I admit is always
evolution from a history.
If it's the revolution that you seek here's
another male peak.
It's the way a man can sound, the way
a man can look,
The way that in the mix fluidity took
time and the dj's in rhyme.
It's not to bleak. I've already succeeded
in leading the blind to a better time
Learning it's impossible foreseeing and
now I never fell I know I'm leading.

This renegade tempo in control of the
solo bassline, beats and all melodies
Within the once spherical envelope
complete me.
Never over analytical is how you please
me as a fan you know I stand
Final physical recipes in the making
from this emcee's hand.
You know the score and international
limits are other boundaries links
Between the way everything is here to
stay and yesterday will make you think.
I can handle this, like any game I insist
turning the groove making dancers
twist.

VI

Sequential are the feelings in this list
hyper active is the best way too to
admit.
I'm never out of it but always rave a bit
gathering our dancing like a mist.
Habitual mind of mine always in the
mix. Reasonably fortunate a future is in
the distance
Energetically guessing but to where
we're all moving at a chance.
Friends realised not just my living is
advanced. Enigmatic as I pass new
independence
Real evidence is my score, no sonic
imbalance. Actual interference from a
different world
Leads to incredible levels of existence
undisturbed.

When I cannot remember a specific line
my mind has said.It is as if a ghost has
moved me to another purpose. Am I
blessed? I write throughout a time
when I am stressed

And back to fundamentals higher learning is my zest.
Every other day I have to wonder if I'm best in a game of illusion
I just have to make the grade, vital I take the test, an infusion confusing to the average body, why?
Don't settle for less! Overtones monotonously sighted make me exited.

With so much going on I am delighted, fortunate always within my actions smooth, running away.
Another sweet hypnotic groove, mild my sector will improve.
Occasionally set out of step but never out of fluid in this jungle getting wet.
I select renditions which ultimately never loose. Even in the roughest conditions carefully chose rhythms.
Respect is a feeling for your heart with pure visions, less inhibitions than more religious missions. I think what we're feeling right now should be the solo.

I value in a tense cause I'm not
practised sober...
Roll over, I must be high or on a dare
this ain't no errand, Love is the reason
for the words here.
Occasionally so commissioned never in
error. Do you really need the rest of this
desire?
Or did you know? Narrow pretence
reasonably on show coordinated
overseen enabled.
I just wish that I could slow myself,
instant record, digital, rewind and see
how I go down
Re endure my image for practising
purposes until I'm through. Getting
bigger
Collecting a plan straight out of the sky.
Leave the world wondering why.
Although now I realise what I do will
never be despised. Cause I'm the
quickest, shortest, thinnest, wickedest.
Around, as a dj goes I've always got a
new sound.

I'm here with a reason ideologically I
have the proof
I never ever wanted to scare, although
this is not the only tension.
It's clear that I'm going to care in my
advent of creation.
Meanings radical for truth so strict my
wickedest session.
Section in successions I invent a dilution
specially here, a new introduction with
a system
Intent realisation. More than a clue
specifically diagnosed the trip solution
radiates and moves.
I still have to know if it's OK really there's
been no destruction, almost completion
nearly
Coordinated clearly do I want to remain
severe?
Indebted not to evil any exampling just
Love. Enough to share,
English how I swear sampling adjusted
I am there.

I could've thought for you, I've got to think for me, what a necessary task each time to believe.

Remained static from above every known face any similar place just resting a case.
Near from the past is how it sets into grace no immediate confusion the entwining of a lace.
So if force is low an answer's easy as a taste for a minute, I thought I was the best. It's just a race.

It's my rage even when I fade my truth's invading no finer days indeed inside this gaming.
Now my future's logic so far entertaining and rocks it.
Making me never ashamed what I've chosen is amazing.
Don't block it. In a past such a blast is so confronting in time overcast is saying nothing. Don't blush.

Immediate and delicate when I'm
rough I know I will touch.
Ever special foundries in a mist no forfeit
much.

Rap is roll, life is Love, passion is sex and
sex you all know.
The pressure of the world has been in a
swirl out of the flow.
But it was when you were sleeping
they'd have taken your soul.

These lyrics here have no reason to
offend, I'd offer to a friend how I feel
Because to get into life can be so real.
What we can afford is to often be
Natural for the actual scene so gradual,
I'd rather slowly smooch than I'd have
to try.
I see the insight in my mind and
through my life is always.
Digital hoping we touch historically
clinical. So I've been blowing,
Thought into another subjects possible
I'm not just quoting my own emcee.

Cause I can say enlightening evidence
that's so uplifting.
Passing places far and near in a system.
I'm a victim I may find no
Higher sense when I'm in collision.
Diction through out my up bringing,
Never short I don't try to be out of
order only ever hardcore.
Even though erupting the revolution
seemed to be jumping without
Any drugs in my head would have
been thumping but on top is positive
Function addictive I don't know but
how it's lead is as smooth as
The tail from a supersonic jet. High not
expensive communicating how
We get thinking no regret. Is
quadraphonia out of it yet? I'm just
As mellow as it ever seems to get. Why
forget my mission in the music
I Love to keep making you wet,
dancing rather than using in a listen
able set.
Respect to my sisters and dream team,
following occasional.

Fantasy so you can see we are the beat, never less.
It doesn't make a lot of difference to anyone else what I do when I'm on my own.

I may express or think at times of how it all feels even if I'm all alone.
I like being out, raving or just drinking pints I'm never low
For anyone that needs to know. Within a warmth a special glow.
Having to keep this music clearly for show, an intro escalates as I create,
Make fate. Happy hardcore invented for the way we relate.
When I realised my future on the turntable my birth was the only sure date
I just design another mix and hope that it is rated. The input still great.
Sometimes I may feel I may have to make a break and that is that
I'm not too slow. Although there's no excuse I'm ready to go.

So now I know what's rolling I've vowed never to act so proud
Unless I am seen by my positive agreement and paying routine.The audience. I've never been green but never needed to be ignorant.
I'd like to live for the scene and take care of all of you...
I'm that social hyper gap exchanging letters too fast
Can you learn what I mean cause I'm a bomb
This pictures never wrong and what it might be
Pure as your delight another inspiration for what should be a new song.

Maybe of course in our lives we are the devil. What level?
Can be explaining how complex most of our minds are as we revel.
I offer complicated treble just to settle most of my brain's functions
I'll not always be at this junction, sedated I fly, scattered.

Like a re written anagram in sections, a mirror's reflection
Steady but devious. Close to the ground is where I've found.
No obvious clues in breaking the sound scaled chaos it shattered.
Behind me the memories through what has been scheming
Beckoning dreaming choosing engulfed believed
Concealed to form all of my life in front of me.
Or abrupt call it a pastime through signs and lines, numbers and letters.
Linked values arranging always better every time since the last yesterday.
Yet increasing strength is force you can feel
Super active. Design of a threshold digital and for real.
A night like tonight is the deal.

Right now, I can feel what has got to happen, to make my dreams real

And my lover's dreams real. Life is stronger so I never will be wrong
This is not necessarily final but an actual deal sealed with every kiss the words in my song. From another place auto confirmation is this statement radiates in an infrastructure perceived.
Over sub sequential articles to be believed, messages in this emcee are better to be seen
Mostly old school routines. Anagrams of the last hype mean everything
Ranging from a keep sake to the digitally long section extended. Morals amended.

If you get like I do with feelings that are ultimately new, begin a cycle
Over a call for survival since true no misadventure needed
Imagination selected I don't force feed it vital spirits and actual rhythm to be believed.

Beyond the diagnosed aired are considerations freed super colours and diagrams a strategy
Beat happy nucleus from a never ending recipe
Re numbered moon symphony in a dialect ever ready.
Still steady is this game on a schedule always changing, never the same, always warm.
Never cold on this plain a guaranteed breeze
Is how I like to greet as I may warn my morals rule.
Confused you must have the mind of a fool
Remember this, a thousand basslines will insist. The ultimate breaks in the place is a hook. The dancers cook and melt as the venue shook a pastime like this should never be mistook.
For any terrorist action or related stated here is a list.
No bombs at the function where electricity flows

As minds in the know mix up rhythms that fathom your hearing
Fashions so searing the alternative dance force adhering
Ending as we finally wear out, no doubt here, this is this.
Because of the way I've always looked back on life like a memory, it's not a curse but déjà vu.
The other side just too taboo it might sound funny that I've lived my life right through.
To a subsequent core and I want more operating language how I score. I am the door.
Just like a force ascending never am I pretending some things are large as I enable any ending
Such a lot has been so real in my life I can reveal I've learnt nerves of steel when I've needed to deal
With achievements straight from my heart. From my mind, my soul, the only serious start. Molecular objective what this dj plans to prove

Through out the ordinance higher circles never loose, in the chaos we cruise as my emcee choosing tricks realises that it is smart together in the mix.

An old school recipe designed to educate people in their youth.

If anything is difficult anticipate our move.

Topical my essay as refreshing as a tropical stream.

Here energy is clean, some drop out of life into abandonment so mean.

Sectional relation not opposed to how I have to write.

Insight always trading, saving, taking what I like. Subsiding is nice, reality a vice as sharp as any knife.

Alive and kicking some beautiful advice reorganised safely on any night

And anyway the reason why I Love, because I'm right.

Delivering anything except hate. I've got to teach, I would be able to reach the highest hype

Tonight I'm operating but it's late, declining us each. Defining a fate, logical a coincidence let's make. Identical electrical similarities no mistake, the wheels screech.

I'm scared that I might loose you, cause you know that I have those dreams. I'm learning a routine.
But to you, yes, what could this mean? I know I'm asking questions that are spacing out this scene.
Because we're obviously seen but we can work as a team.
I want to show you my instinctual beam besides this don't you trust it or you think that it's a scheme
Under development I have to secretive the coded screen military inhibitions below us.
Moralistic interaction behind, I want to tell you more I must have told you some
Speaking directly to your mind.

Independent artificial my own dj, my own emcee.
Naturally contrast, a coherence in demand, a fantasy.
Falling in Love is never easy to do because every time that I seriously think I can only rap to a beat.
Now above is often complete, my revival no mystery in fact everything that I've planned is this neat.
True that the chemicals here could be a heat year in year out I've got a tune you'll never doubt.
Let yourself see. Understand forgiven melodies
A traction it is still true within energy, released force from me,
Within an action if you can't argue, agree.
If you're my inspiration now what am I to do?I've seen a future it is optional I care so I have been through
Theories, always lead me back to where I always am, acclaim only due from the reasons in the plan.

172

It's just so true, time is in my mind what are we to find? Inside such delicate mysteries

After intricate decisions attractive inhibitions past inventions in hi-fi make me laugh.

Now I feel justified, been beaten for what I should say back on top form today realise my problems

Without a word in my way I've got to try and state this or my stress will surely stay.

This second predicament happens each and every time that I awake

I have to wonder who I am and what my dreams take.

Or may take, at least I'm not fake and next time I'm back. You will say, for God's sake, and Love all the music that I make.

Confirmation is what I seek, moral checks casual, Behind me a fight to survive more than actual. Some might have made mistakes before but you've got to adore.

The feelings anytime in your heart or in the realm of the senses.
I know that I can settle any mention in this raver's rap dimension
As sections, information an adventure of protection.
There are times when I wish myself into introduction
I believe, that maybe it's not just a flaw, more a new tradition, I've felt this before
No easy selection leads me with a core leaves me with what I see and I saw
Always indicating what the hell it's all for.
At first I feel I can see a hundred years, or hundreds or a thousand
Or thousands, and dreams of as we exist anyway, this is life.
I get confused and concerned that something's not good.
As if I should, I'm on the edge again tonight.

Wheels have been turning as my mind is always learning. Displaying tactics, getting over any drama this might say. I'm not the only one at the gates of Heaven surely. Far away where it might rain this journey is a story.
Relative every day successive mentioned patterns exclusive intimate material so truthful selective magazines on the scoop here is the proof. Settle into the future I use.

I'm always out to convey how I feel even though at the moment not having much is really the deal
And I try to stay on top. Entertaining sensual demands I never stop.
The freedom in my life has never ended although cloudy this rhythm has mended
Cultures that were once believed so simply I just don't want to take a note of what's offensive.

In vicinity laying down the only method
how I'm standing tall cause it's
defensive
This weapon is repeating as intended
and now that it's befriended, a stated
so rendered
Continuing my plot for unity. Settled in
amongst a new surrendered territory
blended. History can never be deleted
but I'm out of time with hip hop.
Under stated, we rave and collect I'll
never forget.
It feels so cold sometimes to know the
score and roll I've got a soul, and now
I'm not afraid
Left with all I have created in a test zone
I could tell you everything.
The past and the new things. Traded
not jaded, reminiscent, always fadable.
Truthfully cravable, nobody's unsavable.
Do you really think you're so good?
Never misunderstood,
Etcetera, and excellence had naturally
been on everybody's side

From the first high surf reflected by the tide. Just some more things you fail to understand

As grand as planned as a genius would need to know majestic, any coding never slow.

Completion so the sight is digestible realistic, reliable, nihilistic worth every kilo

And recyclable, tolerated so honestly old, good as gold, undefeatable.

Hectic this scandalous knowledge superior the wearier past is deleted, maybe

I come to terms with the fact it will never be repeated.

Rules come first. It is a world where law is a version of what should in a method stay related

Toyed with, fascinating in my mind feeling fated, new excursions not bypassed why trait it?

Coincidental as of late is that great.

Recovery, no urgence is the state of this

emcee. Deliverance, exposure of a guarantee.

Things have not been the same since I self learnt the game.

Times have changed, now with what I know I have a style to match my character and name.

My ever beckoning fame, catch the links through the design of my chains.

I will remember again. As I need to impress

Leave undiscovered pain fulfilling a dream is not my only aim. I have to wonder in my life am I the soul blame?

Rephrasing parts of my knowledge till I'm sober that's what it's for, the lines until it's over. A legitimate price I pay to get my head this way of this formula there ain't another, discover

A range so big and now again I'm sure it is the only constant manual with a foresight almost holy

Everything I do severely mental and why? To stay in the game and get by.

My head the impresser, confessor I
don't lie. Decisively narrative and
centred, in time
I may tire but at first I am a fire. Wicked,
my second is signs.
My third is sense, my fourth is rhymes.
Through which is desire not learnt but
always intended to be meant
Delivered as a trial, infinite
correspondence for a while.

I'm not cheating when you know my
mind is repeating
There's no defeating I've always been
achieving and still a detectable level is
reached
Since the first search I have learnt and
become believing. It's what I've lived,
my mission is invading
Since I've met you a new inspiration
happens to be gracing truly
complicated arrangements blamed
Evidence has the fame so I continue
these games. Re embracing solutions
memorable

Synced into real life as previously
discernable untraceable, slowly
interested more in darkness
Here is the force now test the
sharpness. undeveloped so a power is
waiting to be used.
Nearly represented in lines as a juice, an
ultimate root, terminal velocity is such a
speed to suit, at any cost my reasons
are a youth.
How would you like it if your life was
falling through not sure what to do, in
control of people
Who are not afraid of you, I don't know
where to start although my dreams are
clues.
Safely always thought that I am good
news I'm still confused because we
know I'm pushed
And now my full force version should
be more than enough
You see I have a point to break, since
lovers so fake

No new ideas here I take. As old as the hills passing of thrills. Together can we chill?

Don't you know I believe in a deeper life
On the other side to this natural sense we have our dreams
Where we perform our fantasies.
It is only getting up in the mornings which gets me through a scene.
Feeling meanings far inside, is my mind clean? Never been this way before
The further it would seem I get past all the more
Discoveries fleeting since another chance meeting on the other side I wonder, my heart beating
Never cheating my soul's realms, time itself
Rebuilding as I shock in defence through a past that's locked.
Acceptably sealed, socially sectioned.

No misinterpretation here I mention

Inventive connections as I've serious justice in selection. Morally developed intentions

Our accuracy, mainly in dimensions, a location

For today's race age information. Dedicated revelation.

Transmissions not fit for the children of this nation although we can't hide you can tune to a station.

Such a beautiful lift my life has now felt I wait while it's happening through time image pelts.

Consistently confused although my big-beat will belt my other emcees melt.

Vicious never is the place where dreams are made this symmetrical quest forever making the grade.

Decisive, on the mix I've always been the trade defensive; with myself I am the fade

At least the way this travels I must say beyond usual particles I generate everyday.

Sincere as immediate option to create
the waves scientific disposal in a
sequence
Saved are such solemn scriptures
rewritten occasionally. I don't want any
victims!

In another area I'm questioning
agreements full intention to have seen
it, already methodically toxic
A reasoning beyond the diagnostic.
Which at a cost is how I vox in a
streaming light.
Magnetic, suggestive back across with
what is changing.
Too true, a calm nature seems to suit
the relentless.
As we enter, never aging, my
procedure never senseless, new
plaintiffs panoramic as an energy.
Extensive, if things are around the other
way it's sensitive, do you relate to this
data I may say?
So obviously trying to be right, another
hype sedative

Organised narrative, settled, corrected,
arranged. Again I pledge sincerity
synaptic courageously in full range
Understated moralistic perfectly stated
never vain
In charge of a force as strong as a train
unless, I won't fail my fashion, I'll rave
again.
Riding with me is as far as I see a safety,
I say, who is he? I'm only normal
Looking, here I may be superior. To see
close
I'm never the most terminal ghost on
top as I relate the post.
Reality supposed diagnosed just as
vogue
In deep, seduced. What is the code
behind the way you move?

VII

Virtual coordination lacks in no flavour this behaviour in fact attacks a point enduring me, a raver. At advantage like my area in a space I've seen wearier. Now clearer suggestive still to share, remove the barrier. Factors try to scare me when really you're now near me. I've been a freak, ultimate ideas as my realisation peaks. I'm going to speak of which I've been seeking relief within discretion, followed never weakly

Uniquely spaced balanced as the wax is weaving my study has been solving problems so neatly

Difficulties I now glide through completely. Boundless un empty renumbered entity.

Guarded by no hypocrisy on a level now across eternity as one.

Reasonable, I always like to sketch out event horizons. Giving up the crack through all virtuous reasons I am back. On time another spree of balance straight building I stack.

Confirmed still introducing from the pack, a latest stock.
My letters rock over the best with minimal shock
Full range frontier converging on the line, never a mock.
Binding blinding reasons I'm increasing my learnt version from a prodigy, instant as a road block
A skirmish with sinister intent is what we meant
Dangerous what we may want if we stop, it's the ozone lock.

To list it my dilemma I have to state dangerously dubbed, have I been missed?
The intentions in a mist again leave other gangsters quizzed.
Poetic moments adjust the drift, I will always trust in this gift.
If I am patronised I can break dimensions down in a rift.
In epitome seduced securing any memories loose I can admit.

Vocal passages lift originally dark material from a pit, so explain this massively coordinated organised exquisite self defined revival so I can say that I'm fit.
How many understated places do you relate to as I pass.
Specifically only what my audience may create
If one thinks that it is the last laugh, remember I am fast.
Always on track filling in the gaps forever on the make recognised at last.
Well, I've been working with momentum since my first grasp, God, reality, modern world facts
I can lead a clarity in a shape that is no mystery forever without an end a new simplicity.
An attack on the after effects of the classical
Schools for thinking, acknowledging actions and achievements

Altering belief through patterns of fashion I'm not bitter just divulge in a section, a sanction.

Honest because as far as I can see, my mind's the key.

Upon a new sweltering heat .The beat completes melodic rhythms mechanically sleek, invariably a treat.

Always reasonably sweet here are my prospects

Too true since I got rest I have to find all that I use and inject.

Clear the distance connected by respect corrected, I value my effects, many but not enough to forget.

Corporate urban style side show is how I've let my routine go still better what I get.

For an infinite arrangement my stage design is set. I'm never going to knock this explanation and yet

Fulfilling a debt, understood my equation of faith I bet,

Considered I instruct versions of higher intellect.

A journey still fresh in my system I'll rely on any intuitions show I apply from it's true roots.

All ways favouring my specific tools, too fast to loose not giving the game away as I use and I choose.

Coded, in my memory and mind diagrams, sequential logic behind the fabric that we're flying on

New and higher plans, an optically bright stand

Not really liking what so many have to say but in this land

Everyone's going to realise you're just pretending because you can.

Born again tonight, a vision clear in sight, no vicious delight

Of the wide angle capturing a beat coincidental, dedicated

Every function escapism. Gradually a heat, generally a vacuum.

Is it exposed what we keep? Or safer than next week.

So there are books upon the planets,
on the Earth but what is it worth?
Things are so big!

Like inspected by insects observed not
just by our words modulated, in space
it's so real I can feel
Minute by minute twenty four hours a
day how else can I say.
Never making a meal is the case and
anyway.
I can breathe, imagine you were just
cut off in space left to decay.
Where would you get? What would
you say?
I need an instrument to play generating
an equation, for everything an
explanation.
Setting in the cleverest vocation still
scary. Beyond virtual realities, commend
them to a friend
Eventual bad information, super
information just no end.

Excuse me but why'd you ever shout
the wickedest is never doubt how a
feeling gets about.

How it all works, casual but bezerk
chaos isn't wrecking
This is the way that it's heard, constantly
observed.
Natural energy specific words for
curving I've got tricks
Mixed, I'll be missed when I'm gone,
where am I from?
Veils and screens to be only seen
through. Personally incredible
Belief in the all new, it's never through,
fantastic on queue.
Floating it moves, not out of a time this
vessel ballistically rude.
Automatic magic in simultaneous
groove.
Now I understand what I need to
progress is a studio/lab.
This ain't a fad, I can stay on top of
what I need coordinating constantly
changed lines in procedure

Pure electro feed. So many deeds. Will you endure?
My public must try to play my sounds, because I've found.
As I declare that our hearings around a new turn astral terrorist in a shift. It'll get around, bound.

To blend, a serious happening new hardcore to the ground, trend.
I was stuck on until I realised the potential, incidental.
Unseen cause of power fundamental. I can live my life with ease
As aged sentinels look down onto my needs, my reasons and beliefs
Like the mountains my achievements behind me at relief.
Passages and various travels so content me at least a lasting tease
Hypnotising visions not of dreams, in the sky a message of big words.
Aligned as if the Gods have revealed ancient rules in a circle.

From a language like swords to a never ending fire almost certain.
I can maintain with rhythm methodical, spelt out is no curse.
Are my eyes an act of anarchy? I always look first.
This is for other people who might be living their lives deep, it's how I serve.
My mission is a relative companion, standard action, my ability a choice
Interpretive passion in a centre was a noise of completed fashion.
Now is the angle as I organise any arrangement by status.
Repeating vows my programming is a credit to the nation.
Relentless economists will pick out my style and cry ovation
Super information, was this invented by me?
The latest station for physics in relation carried through like a stream.
A graduation various levels can accept just what I mean.

The reason why I hatch a plot to convince my conceivable following I'm never borrowing anybody else's lines, I have the time.

To compose, circulate living revolving around signs unlocked.
A message rocks. I have to take the looks I have to unwind and block. Feelings that I don't need away from me, no shock reality and dreams complete my certainty. Any angle that I choose through a higher destiny arranged as I'm still taking what I took. Ever regular meanings considered every day I am no crook. Decisive portrayal in design forming an identity hook.
Intent is what I do, intense, intensively made to manage is this major force introduced to the crew.
A new magic under remote control from my hand. Just once maybe my life should be planned

Ultimate bystanding is no way to include how I do since I became a man.
Never through until the day I die this emcee's truth intensifies.
Do you hear that I can? Whenever I'm in practice I am the session.
Understand?
Still multiplying what's fine mixed up just on time, I used to worry
With outrageous implications, but underneath I always knew what to do.
Learning at a raw degree symphonic sophistications.
In a style here I'll still try to cram synthetic although authentic publications.
Steady as my mouth or my mind will let me create in fluctuation.

Time has no beginning for last places, new faces predetermine how I act.
Virtual fact is always changing socially grading sinister internet not plaguing,
Some saying double amplified dating any recreation, just a brief.

My control considered marking how I
start
Drum rolls accommodate this mission
from the heart of possible narration.
I finish when I could really use a type
writer from hell and tap all night.
New radiation into the future with
cunning, no slumming I'm happy.
Seducing what's coming. A full drop
incidental like honey not funny.
Serious if I connect to an interruption,
am I upset? With blank respect.
Sometimes I can move but I'll never
forget the reasons in every.
Second spent on high intent, my sober
set collected for effect.

Alienation of subjective separations, I
don't want to know,
Feelings that I've had before had never
had the need to be slow.
Teaching religiously more, frequently at
hand to be adored ever within narrow
moments are the force.

Realistic, I drop drama and interesting course minding righteous, no dilemma so far impeding what's dextrous.
Infamous our imagining of space, my rendering through time, down finding in this race a start.
Not taking what is mine you're listening to the lines
I can pull apart where light is dark, where sound is smart.
Gathering recognition of an art, incentive calmly wise.
Hesitant for a reason approaching the most. Too wide, my attitude synonymously I boast.

I have the truth in my possession, by all means remaining
Still focused and blaming, changing as I get past what is staying.
Residual information precious playing in the form of records,
Every motion forwards almost a static representation.

Actually I'm never bored, it's worth a mention little known invention of the millennium relaying
Functional beats that revolve. Standard inspirational studies that dissolve.
Under taken frequently so honestly never planned in this vital detection.
Coordinated swiftly and then followed in relation a single knowledge from the arms of creation.
Edited, sometimes memories pass me by at a junction dedicated I won't overlook a sly intention.
Reflections of laughter, comedy and tragedy, mysteries seriously mentioned
As attractive, forgotten are connections variously simultaneous my condition reactive understood
Energy replenished, unblemished, actually good.
This ain't too sad, I've been bad. So I've lived to deliver the radically mad.
Traditionally I'll set the pace from a plan in graduation, the pleasure you've had

Is a beginning of creation. Since all knowing this seamlessness is showing Formulated to be passing not your level I'll indicate a massive fad.
At my pleasure, secrets synonymous and crafted into black
Forever at disposal in an order we're all choosing then it's back, in the track. I will continue just until the emcees realise.
A catch that don't fantasize. It's this world's real lives.
Remote control designed with every action of the soul in mind.
Known now to be so digital, correcting morals, I'm cruel to be kind.
Overwhelmed I recognise a sense to remind I myself of the find
Although it is neutral at this time, like a friend, a safety sign.
Whenever vital, all you may need are my lines. Gravitational feelings are alternative always behind
That is why I believe, can't you see I'm still achieving?

My style is so fresh it leaves the schemers dreaming
So fly my message just chills out in the sky politicians every day can wonder why
Everything I learnt at school gets me by. Revealed sophisticated sinister to start a revolution, who'd try?
Understanding now how people look at me, I've got to state this major dictionary.
Functions and reasons design their own destiny it is fresh to see, how do I do it? Still a mystery from an industry.

Or a point of view beyond such a positive strategy. Electro, new wave, big beat, drum and bass, it always helps to communicate.
Hear the finest. Composed to persuade you to take up their relation
As anyway such a combined power this all makes I could never flunk this suggestive narrative equation

Always the prospect of crossing the
answer lines is so soothing
Forever improving often winning never
loosing. Every attempt at beginning any
fact is sixth sense choosing.
Why do I not quite realise when I might
as well keep my options wide
I like to design, formations of sonic
illusion I don't need to turn the tide.
As a raver I'm observing taking versions
and through the night
Volumes to distinction no fiction I have
realised. Justification of the vibe I'll
always like
Concentrated centred conveniently
burning bright.
Love is the law when the feeling's right.
Coordination
On a level is the score, why be sore?
The future's out of sight.
Cool, calculated, what I hear is
mediated now you know it's only so
through diagnosed serrated
Places, distinct separated optional,
collated

You will never forget such a style on display. I must have made it!
Superstitions sometimes to the hilt and in reverse
It is just the same, don't milk too much this highly lit advice.
The juice is in a burst, a game and now again I've given it away.
I Love to say, I'm joking as I'm smoking. What a way to stay.
Under instruction my energies are focused, outlaid,
For the sufficient prospect of significant fame, I'm amazed.
See I'm always paving the way to a more peaceful day.
And as I say, you will realise my creations never fade.
Saving which makes sense in every episode obeyed
Checking any plans for entertainment I have made
Big and as bad as the secrets that I trade, now who's afraid?

All eventualities understood until my grave. This is the game.
Other rules have been added but it's basically the same.
This area I have under control will never age. Our science insane
The evidence before me itself is so strange, radical visions.

Belong to memories everyone has in their brain.
Still, no stereotype images will ever get me through the pain.
I was there at the beginning and I'll serve you again.
I'm not ballistic with attitude just decent to remain
In this sustained class, a premeditated task. Any fans I must thank.

My mind a mirror no lie with my life a shimmer reliably delivered concentration my deadline

Closer, bigger almost on top of what is next
A motion's revolving, dancing in step, talking in rhyme, acknowledging effect
Choice with no regret letting voices simmer, only a winner can relate to the latest signs
No, I'm not a beginner. Technical achievement from my brain for entertainment is fine.
Reckless information is a strategy, the weapon and guns are in the sky, a high profession
Carrying on with the blessing, no disguise trusting in the rules of my lessons I must try.
Measured symphonic data always getting us all high.

Understood, if I was dry this position would not exist so instead I couldn't mix, I won't persist,
To enlighten as I can I'd grow to resist.
Happening reaction a formula I admit and the advantage of whit so lifting,

velocity on show, I will explain how I know. Just a gift, energetic beyond slow.

Now for once, I'm admitant, in a flashback the keys to a situation brand new

I can explain anytime this hip hop game. It ain't been easy, before I was stoned I get confused

But my life needs me. Needing to be quicker I refigure past times like a dictionary

With each and every explanation finely singular and very real.

I feel. It's nineteen ninety eight this is the deal, desire to produce

Information also truth while I'm a youth, a certain drive from a time that you wouldn't believe

It ain't no hype or drive I seek, these morals creek, besides myself if I speak.

Remixing juice. I can't feel down this frame of mind obtained believed unique.

Drums always should remind me I'm
that clique, escape of the bleak
Refuge beyond quick my search
automatic, mimicking any platinum
plated break
So conclusive are the peaks reached,
accelerations are complete
Realising it's the misguided causing us
to weep but I'll get by with my sleep.

When you die maybe all that you see
are your dreams, like a high,
Although life can be mean there's a
definite schedule forever a line,
Permanent a structure referring time.
Studying ability which divides.
Stereo features of a future style, I'll be
relying.
Foretelling not indifferent implying my
multimedia siding up to frontiers.
Smiling and into prototype years,
blinding richer methods tear expanding
never gambling.

Sober in a tribute I can engage
managing, owning in on which I never
over analyse,
Subscribed in a way emerged this
remedy I'd navigate localised while
things are numb I'll rearrange.
Climates are crossed conditions with
held it's hardly strange
Sonic vocation in complete
containment in my name.
Guess my game, I'll never drop a point
and enter three letters quickly on the
hall of fame. It's insane, never tame,
about but I'll be back again.
Instant satisfaction but I have to attempt
to break these chains.
Feeling ambiguous is steady again,
repeating no phrase.
This converging gaze is the many
answers needed to the maze,
Entering the following stage there is no
pain automatic grace.
Distinct velocity a chance, remembered
in advance before I get too far I am but
peaceful in a trance.

Unknown vicinity, eternal numbers,
bracketed hyphenated checks,
Sometimes it's just not helpful to forget,
so simply wrecked.
Partly as a set for listening peers as I
select correct reflections,
Adequate soulful ambitions, tailless
demands are the commands.
Recently atoned versions through
stone, no fake mechanical,
At all, surfing tall, with an identity
creating a new wall,
For it's own foundations the collection
is never alone.
And repaying scales known is truly
chosen beyond a zone.
Classical mutations only take me further
through directions that attempt me,
Well led transactions surely respecting
how we're getting.

Any letting across is sophistication as
energy directing when inventing I'm
back together at some entry.

Level, area inside haunting me never turning around.
My serious investment in any case, still momentum as a key.
I can recognise the images in anything, pictorial, actual.
Will the possible list of icons involved ever be fact? Or a machine made of pieces rectified in the need
For understanding will rule before there's a chance to concede...
Questions brought upon from lessons in speed. The birds and these bees are safely explained by me.
In my life a real time complex through which we all came to be.
The first sinister attraction leading meanings into the free.
Now what'd you see? What's the point in living if you don't want to breathe? Air and I need.
I thought I knew how to behave and at least

I'm always polite, I've never lost it, that must be why I'm boss of it don't need to be cruel.

I admit I'm in control of this circuit, time is something else for me, But I'll always be serving it's chemical advice. It is important.

I should be writing down the tunes I need when I hear them on the radio, statistically a cross section

Of hype through out the years in tasteful stereo, altering our minds with shade.

To a better lifestyle recycled rhythms play.

Remixing produced for the parallel dimension, castle mathematics

For the latest generation, respect, in grammatical quotations.

I've got to log some informative seed for the future in sections so I'm sure of matching expectations. Anyway I still practice. How could you be afraid? Platte rotation edited in formulation, hypnotising loops are made.

Final answers in every fade, except a new beginning the spark accelerating start in another crusade.

So I will, resolute when I must, I don't run from this happening just optimistically bust.

When we're quiet we're at our most dangerous it's a home rule that's contagious,

I'm not just letting on because I'm famous, reckless, maybe, just like what is written

On each and every of my record's labels, never mindless and how did we meet?

Seeking out rhythms, exploring the beat, chasing the dragon. Never in defeat, relaying basslines with a quality to repeat. If I set off a bomb it's just the way that I speak. How not to know. Choose ignorance, choose forgiving. Why worry? How not to bother when what's coming. Is just as significant as anything you can be feeling in existence, this is true as I only advance

into the distance. The force we're
believing is so adult, mature
diagnosing,
Super structures of design from a vault
left you supposing. However it all
started as if by default composed,
revolving.
In code, created evidently since
explosions so old. This article alone
worth it's weight in gold.
Set extensively with all jewels, other
metals and precious stones.
Half of the time I'm left with too many
ways to version,
And only lately are there really fewer
reasons to tone. Are you amazed?
Your average dance floor can heavenly
gravitate
As the weight of the dj's fingers makes
the records moan.
Never been a clone, I'd understand
when I'm alone but all the time I'm in
control, I check the zone.
In the twilight till breakfast, anytime I
can convince you that it's changed.

Why ain't it legal? How can I find peace in this sequel? I feel blamed.

This is the last time for a lot of what's been going on in my life
Should it stop? I have to wonder when I find it's so powerful.
Pure hip hop in life a blur, immediate satisfaction guaranteed.
So like cats we purr, renegade a fashion forced in hype.
One thing I have realised is a location in reality is reflected
That is actual personal reality respected. Connected? I've got to fly!
Some how I never force feed any guy this information never dry.
A design from the mind, lines numerical formulae, co habiting equations list
Digitally complete ideas consist in patterns in a memory programmed to exist
No exit past the borders I admit as many as you need to happen resolving any future.

VIII

Language like an adored gift of angels
or gods here's the proof. Entertaining
hi-fi
Resolute, mixing up biggest clues,
anonymous virtues. No promise missed
Extensively relayed is a steady groove,
while mentors move into this.

Tonight all of my past possessions are
forgiven fast implementation, attractive
in decision.
Recognition of forces arising. Collected
mixing of pre amped career
exchanging and sticking.
Dust never settles when it's covered
intent, ever accurate ideal, in my life.

When ever picking how I feel,
choosing, cruising in a musical key,
used to involving
Saturated solving whilst revolving.
Recording, imminent progress working
high and dry.
Flying ballistic conduct always
consequently why. Concern your mind
with my palace
Incidental, magnetic with a practice a
language maintained lavish.
It took me a while to realise, obviously,
sixth sense I'm not opposed to
What I trust, but in the rush, I must
have missed just how scary.

A concept can get in my reality as such.
A versions alway's new.
Explanations are due so an actual
understanding follows through.
I try to match, scratch scheduled
intentions, versions often burning.
Earning as I mention a finer reputation
always deserving.

Now you can see why my minds been hurting dodging and swerving, causing and serving.

Rivalistic particularly clear, I hold points that endure higher fear
In nocturnal surroundings, groundings had announced a presence,
Crowded, surreal hung a temple witnessed by thieves.
The anonymous believe but this can settle what's been found.
Gods in their mysterious habitat evolve, royalty had solved
Passionate consolidation through chapters of old.
Countries, cities, futures and events fore told, the most mystic.
Adaptation of logical systems only a toy. But you're going to know.
From an order of no choice unless you listen enough to your own voice.
You wonder, am I part of all this? Is it all part of me?

Never get chemical imbalance from a man that can't see.
Understanding my main step around and beats fashioned on electricity.

I've decided to have no problem, just underlying talents and emotions.
They try to capture me in frame through transmissions. When is the collision? It is the snare, I'm on a mission.
Openly devoted to the truth, ambitious situations can always take you there, why stare?
Since the curse of a caution I have been aware no final curtain in this stage of life to compare, amidst a quality route with parallels I share...
I couldn't help to notice this, but it's so hard to understand, it's just like how we.
Used to talk, not different from how we can. For the future I have planned availability.

217

Through operands, individuality in modern jams, new coordination particularly precise,

Really the new vice, cause if I'm honest it's hot my material but not borrowed. Bothered?

It's why I've got to stop and drop anything I'm doing just to maintain this loud narrow.

In between wild thing, I'm honoured. I discovered in the first place the earliest traces.

Of primeval race, emergence like rage coming to terms with itself at no other stage, learning.

Comprehension, another page, since the weird beginning to the completion of a phase. We are now living in the days of a technology craze, anything you need and smaller.

In your life to be graced, faced once with the question user friendly now advertised,

On the telly every four seconds something trendy. Just how creative do you think.

The real population are with this eternal brink I'm wondering where is the sense in this link?

Obviously, well even the sky has a ceiling so, practical I'm conceived and already believing

Seeming like everything has got a meaning of course so now cease your dreaming realise

Quantities of formulae, realities exercises with it's edges forgiving you and me in style

Because I'm concise always time to get wise here's the file, entertainment on a tile.

Any adjustment has got to be forward, rules so figured in my mind never bored

Expansion of a sort, hardcore.

I can always expand my limitations, racing predictions in imagined quantities

Positions, in my dreams, prescriptions,
descriptive only positive collections.
In a matter situations literally no obvious
denial of formation here,
Extended on from a previous secure
school never challenged, forever near.
Sometimes it happens recognised
usually clear, vital intrinsic now here.
Instantly mastered, mature and real a
favourite energy I feel.
To rearrange which I am looking at is
the deal
Automatically revealed of course as
available the deciphering will heal.
Even this incredible fast and educated
zest is never a guess.
And next a plain where anything can
happen makes sense
So where's the rest? Buried in the pink
Such a massive multitude compiled to
make my listening audience think.

Because my methods are tried
untested, conditions defied,

Reality purposes described at worst, at last, well anyway, first.

The rap that I can listen to really is the best, it always makes me think,
Now I have survived I take my pick of what's clear and check the link,
Such a massive congress in the area so quick, virtually this.

Lethal land, level lines literally limitless, lasting lessons,
Latest liaisons left listed, language lifting like lasers
Linking leads less letting layers leave little law.
And you thought that I'd be fooling?
I'm not a boy anymore, man, I'm amusing.
Being lazy sometimes can hurt so remain alert, and choosing, days in my life I said are often spent well.

Some things are personal, frequency dissolving, concerning

Their owners of the morals that times bring, the clever wordings,
Of which the beats sing and if it's worth mentioning behind.
Lies a multitude including all possible intentions, even
Less mentioned solutions in a tradition never lost. Still in exploration
This expedition is revealing narration usually on top.
If there ever was a boundary I'd get my mind together and still never stop,
Letting my dj experiment in only the finest drops we grew hip hop.
Cheating? Well me? I'll always choose a fair way I just like to practice. Whenever I can, recycling thoughts
Like lights in the air, ever steady playing it or leaving it to stay,
In the clever, clever rap game.
Self taught is the care.
Dynamics as a standard we just share, in the computer age.
What you need for your faith is inspiration glazed at what may

Phase. Unhesitant mastery of your scene for days and so, even years as that initial investment revalues and pays.

In the stereo test zone I am a dedicated flunky as I warm with my lyrics I make funky
It is bad to be bionic, as bad as I believe with deteriorating life and exaggerated dreams.
Well, I've worried, amplifying pain, analysing the principles that started
My addiction to the game, my want to win and my ability to totally remain.
Telepathy is thinking for two, forever meaning what it knew.
At least, a force that's never doomed, it is planned how I prove,
An unstoppable groove based on science rendered true. Applied and precise
Like yesterday's reality without tomorrow's vice, this natural news.

Sincere relationship, adopting interviews in this fair game nobody's going to loose.

I'll always practice what I choose and preach indiscriminate home truths.

Definite calculation from me invading space in search of higher force and Energies which correspond with my soul and my mind never late in molecular grace.

On vigil my nature I will never forget again to give myself this proper place So perception eternal, perpetual in pace the message from the hip hop days.

This incredible function I've found will amaze. Never written myself out, although

I've often lyrically maintained as if forever at this stage!

Life when we're young, well we thought it was run by politics and laws.

But more then before people have their choices in fun and of course.

Extended pro-active freedom and work is this procedure offered,

In where we've appeared to exist
although only the deeply conscious are
bothered
Weary or worried, conversationalists
and philosophers are hurried.
What is discovered? Surely, and only
the unique sense so withered.
Recovered.
It isn't the impedance of time with
which I find fault I am a wizard
Quartz locked wired science applier
humanely figured.
Harmony buyer, melodies of fire
delivered, nineteen ninety nine has
been triggered
Every real life is bigger steady in a path
sanely quicker.

There are no excuses for this, I had to
think very hard,
Reasons that I give myself are choices
that I specially regard.
Understanding method, approach,
inclination has usually got me far.

Enterprising factually a facility I won't mar, clear like a spar. If elevation from an axis is a spring what will the spirals bring?
Sophisticated, the only way I can sing of course technically construct.
Linked and textured, composed is my voice, just my thing...
Identity for what? Just hanging in the air and then resurfacing
Future proving pure vibes are racing. You've been tasting
Energy gathered through observing in my pattern again I've been lacing.
While I decide my next move a record plays and the memories soothe
Have the nerve to hang around, I am never going to loose.
Effects I've been replacing
Now is the time and it's your minds I have been taking
Information justified intelligence staking, modern groove untill it's obvious there's never been any faking.

Half of this, too much of that, ink only
flowing like a lucky black cat.
Crossing my path I dare to be daft since
my life's been exposing.
Just exactly what everyone should be
knowing. Science fiction makes.
Me want to scream, in conscious
dreams another life has grown.
From a seed. Pasts in my path often
agree, topical, but in life there are still
mysteries.
Like the sun's setting curves and the
curtains of the seas, the moon in it's
orbit,
Pyramids, wars, and future sights to see,
natural evolution through to human
history.
What I see cannot be all, there is so
much happening, life is a mortal coil
A never ending beat focused to how is
chosen. On the screen, digital emotion
Never corroding, often enlightening as
is written in the good book. I'm always
counting,

227

Numbering the prophecy like lessons.
Optional contrast each side of our
space
In symmetry an enthusiastic reaction
surrounds us, so that we can naturally
trust.
Every noticeable event through out my
well being, what I've been seeing
No article unattractive, no particle is left
unaccepted, God is super meaning.
In my position, who can criticise what I
cross or anything that I despise?

Still naturally high as elements collide, I
spend my life correct as I ride
Sympathetic anytime and to the other
side, what we all need is peace,
The radical release of information
which is clear in vibe and pure of pace
Eradicate the habits that have caused
once disgrace, make the change.
Virtual are my limits, hereditary could
be the case, working for the human
race.

On Earth, since my birth from my father
and mother, such good worth
Now how could I have been a mistake?
For the luck of relatives and the chance
on my word
When you understand my tongue is
the sword, make your decision please.
Because I'm on a higher level and I just
seem to hustle any scene.
Language like this with no faults, not
obscene, always clean, gangster's
dream...
Although this experimental quest
became a style, instantly clever my
posse is a team.

Psycho-kinetic like other ravers we have
course, only intimidating other.
Peoples whose belief might be
alternative force, forever sharing
hardcore.

Each time it's ideal, I'm sarcastic I wish I
was taboo and I am! Mixing 'till I fly

No ritualistic enemy or fool dare try, it's
addictive but ranging, cooperative.
Blaming new social circles in events my
occupation will exaggerate as sense
indents,
The planning of my favourite colour
coming over in it's live state.

I cannot change everybody's fate, but
with practice and only a little help
There should be no loneliness as the
lazy lions in the jungle are waking up.
"Stormtroopers", a bionic phase
through with intelligent time a creation
Important is how we live as is
everything we do. Crucial recognition.
This emcee's deciphered by solution,
turning the weirdest interview
interesting.
Methods not to throw far or deviate the
subject are our medium. Since my first
explanation.
The progression here is not unlike a
forest fire. Surgeon's warning,
devastating.

In the area. Not actually much scarier.
Everything that I say one can take two
ways.
The sound of music! Conversations
born from the ripples in time
Static a courageous mastermind, no
fluke, performing, my meanings stand
rebuked.
A colossal disturbance anyway in life
reasoning we've recovered.
Without a common sense the human
race would not have been discovered.
Optionally tangible, essential are my
memories like sunshine's rays and
The human ways. Colourful psycho
active so sober holding together the
land.
Now I am ahead of what I do, indeed
at last no need to disbelieve this truth.
Not written in halves, consequential to
listen to or read, it's so fast. Sincere.

Two millenniums of human nature and
still more, time is always expanding

Through out the universe. Could it be?
Searching inside a meaningless domain,
With super sonic pressures, imperial
treasures and energy to destroy or start
again.
Whims left to the Gods or is it nature?
Massive mathematics clearly visible,
sometimes
Part of a super computers data,
transposed virtual side effects from the
measuring of such vitals.
Original outcomes, comprising fully in
suggestion from beginning to the end
of things... Kind of an adventure, any
page of which is memorable, strategy
invisible, infinite the cradle beyond
Heaven, between our planet and the
stars
Are we waiting for space travellers from
more than what we know as far?
The world's finest instruments, best
mathematicians, professors, unveiling a
new ark.

All of our souls destiny defined by the way we work, walk, tell stories, have fun and talk
In accelerations unseen are the sparks from the grind. Can you imagine? Phenomenal signs are the functional meaning of time. What much more would anyone need to see?
Education is the key, swing at momentum, spun in a web like gravity. Just enough imagination and the project is speeding needing maybe slight
Delicate surgery. Enhance the future, glance back to the past, focus and then rely
'Cause the radiating eminence immediately in forecast is this trance. Solar and cosmic emptiness bypasses life accordingly, a vision so bad.
Either way you're going to have to know that I run the show. Understood, I always knew that I would, starting as only I could.

Diagrams have their sarcastic delay so there's appliance as I say. Speak Through. A cordless dimension stands today with no limitations just go.
Take fortunate situations on a flow for your awareness. Answers to your questions
Before you need to share the fairness in duality a destiny is shaped.
With symmetrical advantages a quest to rock on into fate.

Ordinary surpassed for a system that is great, reasons with a depth to animate.

Because, reality, respect criticised me, I see eye to eye with fire.
Life's a trip, why do I rip? Fingers all close to the nib. Challenge,
God is in the house, I don't need to fall, I have learned
From the most beautiful music in my life which has burned.
This isn't a fashion syndrome but I've got bongos, ballistic feuds,

Just want to make some fun of you, after you, what's the use?
Frustration with the radio on relaying news.

Excited, don't say ecstasy just yet, since a broadening.
Direction of my future's set, emotional this standard tangent.
Floats and envelopes, protecting what I have said, still good enough.
Because time is the spark in the eye of the mind, always in front.
Only so small, the imminent nature of everything again is the call.
Primitive want, energy serving solid as walls where ever my intellect turns.
For modern terms I roar, checking back across the board for what stands tall,
Manipulate the fall, calculating one and all, until like the pitch shift you have a ball.
Can I not be trusted? With what I just did, I can only really remember how I feel

And right now again I've touched it. I must admit my mind's adjusted.
How I walk, the way I bust it, forceful thoughtful together.
We've sussed it, every vision, any sign of course I code these.
Available on time truly delivered relevant applied for a need.
Step into the future believe in what you see, simpler symmetries for destiny
Hemispherically designed creating formulation in deed, only harmony and a beat.
Rare recollections of climates so high, passed days of various ways
Always complete memories every time sweet.
So this is a real situation between politics, medicine, men and women,
Law, refreshing my hardcore. I've felt this before but it never makes me sore.
I'm versioning every thought I have, this is what it's for, ecstasy.

And now I've got to tell the whole
world the score, in of course a
controlled manner.
Incredible to me how sometimes this
don't start world war three
I'm one steady emcee that can't
stammer, lights from my body they
don't see.

Until I'm past the banner leaving
reminders as I can, here is the plan.
Heavy as a hammer smashing justice
into beaten jams across our land.
The problems, sometimes remembering
is hard, that it is all in the mind
Electrical like the travelling of stars,
repetitive bars, revolution of time.
You'd think that I would have enough
moments to unwind, I'm not unkind
With these optical kinetic examples you
will find. I know you know what it
means.
I say, you wouldn't want to see my
writing, it's extreme, like an examination
paper

And I will Love you. But when it's getting confusing I'm having one hell of a time.

I will Love only you. Waiting for the next rhyme.

From a right angle I can see the angels, mental saviours, withholders of nature.

Dinosaurs of truth forever saving the rolling secrets of gods since primeval times

The line of Heaven, gathered by minds as agents willing could. Who am I?

Some are better, some are good, realistically understood on this Earth as I should

Never giving up my prime vital statistic I always would, since a young age

Learn from every page, decidedly each lane, any pain disappeared

Away from my brain secluded in a reality game as I'm naming again

Rave on! Automatic strokes in a remembered chain. Scoring the same

In the hall of fame, only the highest of events gets a mention

Here is a tension. Uniqueness first in sound and then invention
Moving through the situation entering darkness of new dimensions we trip on
Behavioural evolution we don't start from, eventually the few are free
As remarked upon this convenient way to be composed by a gap called infinity.
Why I am a refugee is mostly because now I am not concerned with
How I may look, fashion is the moral for this industry, caught in a dream.
So many things to be, but don't call me Jesus, Moses, Aladdin or Peter Pan
I grip the mic in my hand, everyone understands. Films and movies next
Don't let a sign of power perplex, it's in the can, these finest of jams.
Specialist remedies in melody, once from a boy but now from a man.
Interviews a treat, organised at a schedule, a learning school with a rule
Automatic tools adjust the surface until it's clear as a pool. Smooth,

Radiation improved for desire like a fire, only cool. Played for the mind

Forever true never a fool. God sees me, how can it be too soon?

Another dimension with new intentions I never forget what I was taught, the revelations. Sealed such a mystical weight with such fantastic equations it creates

An asylum in a nature which to any man can relate

Positive forces in the world are not there to meet their fate.

To destroy or be destroyed not really human so I should go on.

Obliterating power to be consumed as a lesson all around shone.

Religion. Religious artefacts of stone and priestly tones from far away thrones

Catch what is kicking deliciously ridiculous I pick this.

The essence of my life are not any victims, I also mix so quick.

Cameras might think I glow, in my
headphone a certain echo.
I'll be the only one to know, the depth
of a category of trance,
Techno, plastic that spins and makes
you want to dance.
Hip period stop forget it nerve is my
curve, adventurous as deserved
When is this repetitive? I have never
heard. Hell how scattered can you spell
any word?
Is this not really funny? As my mind
melts complexities I'm unrivalled.

Apart from Evil Knieval, the bionic man
and top buzz.
The president of the United States it is
fabled, remixes that I've cradled
Hold equations in a situation sky like
forever able, it's a major player.
I crowned, down, only fortunate when
I'm dancing, a raver.
Together hardcore I'm no slower, a
slayer, fastest street sayer.

Still a prayer, digitally delay this if it's available I care right now and later.
From the beginning and again I stay a friend, numerically possible until an end.
Era, generation, period, age, completion of a phase, a race.
Coincidental optimism constantly graced found within a suitable place.

With every breath a shape is created for the next, intravenous with text or complex thought in effect.
Like a rewind, of the mind a spirit anytime scheduled to make sense.
Split up like seconds in a minute but forever a connection, further sections
Adding to the news, foundations in relationship in place spaced through out the case.
No vocal tone can be laid to waste in the clearest taste.

I read about astral projection when I was young, realised it could be fun,

In a free forming galaxy the life that I knew is only one, so I became,
The raver fulfilling my name, like right here now spoken overcoming again.
Spiritual apprehension has never been the same. Will a mogul remain?
Ain't no such thing as pain, my battles effect much attention.
Am I the emcee that they blame? I mostly plan every decision just to entertain.
With a reference, whatever to evenly adjusted my beats bust it.
A maximum guidance line and you can trust it, the sonic rush is so big.
You can remember it's claims, they're always positive, collection in deed.
With connections of need, that's why I pushed it, more for spontaneity than greed.
Hereditary fear must be crushed, my career has advantages, any ambition I possess,

A mere touch, answers in our presence
divine, never too much, good enough
for books,
Taken to pieces by our looks, other
civilizations saw this and shook,
Crumbled to the ground as such,
perished when they panicked then
became part of Heaven intact,
A lesson not to re-enact on Earth
everyday, it's a human price for
knowledge to pay.
Nearer is destruction than politicians
will say.
Since I got rid of the bong I'm back into
the panic, on the narrow lines so static.
Serious no idiot addict remembering
things I actually say scratching with a
technique.
Or similar turntable with plastic as a
magnet I'm still the able agent.
To add attack or decay as only my
fingers portrait, not acting.
Searching, seeking, finding, applying
better known lotions in the mix.

True runnings affordable as the devious sections conduct fresh tricks.

Slower into like snow I can locate the introduction then drop into the program.

At the unstoppable rate, future beats I create. Do you know them?

Highly sophisticated again. I have seen slogans like battlements.

Guns in the sky are not opponents why study them dragons.

Here I'm not bragging, just ultimately capable, fully flagging.

Jealousy always beyond me completes the scene.

I'm the 'I' the 'T', the one you have set free, when you're listening to me.

I am the cause and effect through the light, edited so sweetly in Love Synthesised because we have come from up above, hell, we might be.

IX

The life that we lead, spaces and places
we see, fortune, choice and destiny
Remodelled retextured all for
convenience I am the best of emcees.
Barer of my mistakes I'll never fake, or
produce any flavour insignificant
I dilate, like the pupils of my eyes on
track for the prize
We all win, instantly the slayer of a sin,
don't we all deserve
The luxuries that we think? If I begin so
many sums add up in property,
No negative again, my morals
controlling in the mix, the next link,
However inferior, my method could kid
you I'm a shrink.
If I stop as I'm mid flow it's for a drink
just waiting for the levels to sync
Every time I even start effects assuredly
fast or often quick, always on the brink.

Triple beams I display now are a
fortitude, even, solid
Through static, so fantastic another
mould broke automatically as I did.
I'm in no skid, instant italics arranged
like a liquid, currents lifting
Mechanical it's drifting forever I lift the
lid, faults non existent.
You can question the down beats still
define a situation divine
Flying through time realistic emotion
sublime, underlying into rewind.
This is just what I can handle quite well
at the moment it won't kill me.
Secluded memories may be tempting,
removing me a velocity in circumstance
Fine ultra trance of spiralling tangents
and dangerously deep distances
Of outer space confirmed as listed in
contents designed on the rewind in
advance.
Modulated to be heard in performance
from the stage to it's audience,
This is like a second chance to motivate
a higher romance seen in place.

247

Surfacing again as stars chase this complicated occupancy.
Strange lights in the sky at night time, mean I'm fine.
Circular event horizons are plain to see, soon a fantasy, pre ordained
Will lead the struggle. Through a difference between us and them
And liberty becomes the final line. Avoiding trouble.
Newest schematics on the double, variety a spice
Electrical dice are my favourite device providing power.

Just too nice this scratched CD has been devoured because I play it every hour, taking scratches.
That's what we call it, a game of catch so hot
You've got to watch how endurance is confused until the chemistry states I'm inventing silence
To be used as a tool, in case you needed it to

Here's the dj throwing down the passive rules Like elements to your delight, forever changing.

Moving shadows muse limits whenever improved.

Life is like a candle, all the time that I can handle

My name is four by two, here is a clue, you'd have thought I forgot

I could never loose. Radio-active power don't conclude

The beginning, from the point still a schedule once confused

With a word and system so true, ancient views

Now copied again should end in ritual, secondly I prove

Simultaneous harmonies like stereo move in sight of our eyes

As the night turns to day a mind is wiser and bodies considerably lighter

When delicately placed, crossing the line into grace.

Recording accurately justice misplaced, tomorrows case, a spacey haze.

Through stage to stage a frightening need for blame, I am not the same.
In the human race. Calculated measure leads the rest of the bass.
Juice in a virtual place. At a height and a pace.
Since the first sighting of a saucer, the drum's gathered haste.
Pure logic and chemistry dictates what it takes
Learning the stakes, readiness makes, previous conceptions seem fake.
Overtaking submitting obstacles in a competition like state
Solving God's great gates, the most fantastic fate is delivered.
This is the case, I am the ace, of the ink flowing freely,
Feelings I base, decisions I have made, questioning justice
Coming clean, it takes hip hop people to complete my dream
Challenging reasons may often seem revealing.

Nauseous repeating delicacy called beats through which I am meaning. Virtual vocal picking up to where I'm leading leaving other djs bleeding.
Victory is mine. I've seen the signs back again on time
You actors must be needing all this information are you reading?
Steady organised coordination is a fact, check the track,
Invisible essence this force fulfils a gap, from infinity's tap.
Forever released like a gas, some chemical fast for the rap
Top tactics are engaged so clever I have to laugh as I pass
Definitive endings and moralised flack in spinning black plastic my scratches attack.

I must be passing a space as I laugh after a past full of education.
My friend's narration is clear and anytime forceful in direction sending motion to my ear.

Terminative broadcast fresh this year,
electronics programmed for the real.
Understanding of aware, newly clear
devices aired and sealed.
Released as a display, working
economically I say, on everyway,
No degradation. The art still
challenging salvation.
Interfaced conclusions by invitation
beyond limitation are easy to accept
The only second I regret this discovery
I'll forget
Summarised in many international
alphabets, sparkling in the night sky
when the sun has set.

Through the weird, rude, beautiful. If I
could only travel instantly, I'd Love to,
To inspire. The meaning of life is on fire!
I'll get by and next never retire. If only I
could try
Like I'm trying to remember why I
know, I now realise,
All children are ever taught this
unknown curse so concise

Why tell lies? Sell hell, buy souls, do something different. How could I despise? Meanings in disguise, of infinite order.

Imagined sacrifice burning an individual space and time, dissolving software coded will race.

Corrosion of minds never existed, it's a small world with a lot of names, sheltered games, secretive fame, Something for the aliens or more? UFOs look like they're the score So high in the sky seen to soar. Oblivious to life the heavens darken, lightening and thunder roar. Molecules and chemicals so solid are our door.

But even I understand that a dimension seen by another man can be the other side, the design that the creator did not see

Although his own work he reads, another's ride is high.

Like the beckoning tide completes this schematic rendezvous.

As only God inclines any following rules or alternative moves.
Soothing for the brain of course as through time the mind grows use.
To the new, ever improved, super inspiration included beyond lurid psychedelic momentum introduced.

The negative things that I do are all only positive, as I have inherited my life, how should I cross it?
Safety is a measure in the mind so your soul can be free,
Ain't that just what you'd want to be?
No new routines
Captured in a static scene, the human machine.
Crafted precisely coded so as we remember to breathe.
Honouring my God with the strength of a nod
This verified dream is life as I suppose it
Real super reality won't ever over expose it only the ordinary is in the trap, trip-heads admit

That standard I'll explain so stop.
Pure hip hop.

My emcee's got a lot of advice. Another
virtual aspect.
Is recommended twice, what the
wireless plays is nice.
Forever ripe, sometimes I wouldn't get
by without that hype true and tight, my
favourite dj any night through weeks
and months, I can confront which
some have said is impossible. We'll get
through after primarily stalling for an
interlude.
My imagination can sometimes be so
rude.
Why? Why did you have to let me go?
You know now that we know and so
styles show
I'll always try, now once I had learnt the
lesson sub-tropical clarity with actual
demand I can supply.
Forces of the future, destiny a turn in
nature's rule alternative schemes only
tor the old school

Nineteen ninety nine is the universal proof. How would my sign not be the truth?
Others will be catching up when they latch onto how soothing
Modern drum and bass is moving. Professional boundaries solid surroundings on reference enduring. Until the end of time our free souls grooving. Surviving with what you've tasted, never loosing.

Besides behaviour and such natural player instinct
Automatic and on cue, picking what comes next after I am using.

Ultimate electro. Repeat myself? Built for home cinema on DVD this altogether attitude is cruising.
This ain't an aim to upset, but I can't ever forget
Of history once learnt about, the future now it's met.

Seriousness in the lessons with intent.
Always meaningful on this I now bet
Take a rest. Backing the best. My
reasons are blessed.
Delicate decisions at a crest, I'll profess
not to copy ever more or less.
Any other rap material that I know is
done. These are the unwritten rules
So that we can have fun. Number one,
take note of what the music says
And do it! If you want to, follow
through even though you do.
Number two, I ain't actually listing this,
all that exists is a fantastic view.
Number three, make sure that
everything you say you knew so as it
can be referred to.
Number four, every letter that you utter
will be hardcore, afterwards chill.
It's the vigil overkill. A surge as the
source spills, into break beat taking it's
fill.
Number five, on the microphone stay
alive, like painting, a fire, or the beast
Before it's deliverance to the sky.

Some say places in Heaven always shine but why should I try?
To explain the unexplainable or more if I am able?
Number six, the quickness in pace steadies a state of embodiment so far.

Seven, the message is like a cradle, still heavenly peaceful, together, never far.
Number eight, it has always been fate, I have to follow, of course I can lead.
Number nine, learn to read, the clear methods are like a game.
And if you want it, it is the same, so relax
Number ten now is the time, there's an act so real in life so react!

The song of the surf, could no one on Earth, understand what I manage?
Ecliptic, bionic in stages subsonic. New curves,
A message once printed now has faded, become data dated.

Violated from the present only naturally. Suggesting information, Instant as already recognised, rectified this virtual species
Calling to the sky in obvious frequencies. Deliverance of exodus is All that's on their minds in a study of completeness.
Reality is it all. The final frontier, the spinning wall.
Carefully decided how it's even seen, imaginatively green forever ascending. If generations risk which is mildly sending confusion,
Uselessness may lead to a fall. Strength in the blending of politics.
Separating of halls for gentlemen to respect. But in every actual fact,
Every policy seems to be a trap if it's ever regarded at all.
Promises only in tales kept true, if the leaders of the country are working too Repair will follow to the horizon in view against a Heaven, amidst the blue.

Analysing the beauty of life, I had to
think twice to get hold of myself,
With no maps, designs, blueprints or
foundation, no location so to speak of.
Within verbal vocation once worked,
out. Envisaged the labyrinth called
strife.
But I'm not dreaming, seeming
responsive, I'm still breathing.
Science's ceiling. Our perception in
depth so broad to stay appealing
Revealing connected identified, applied
for a plan, although it's even.
Once the righteous side discovered
winning, the rebels are chilling.
Screaming searches for samples
beginning textured as filling.
Check my skill, information has been
spilling, basslines to kill or mix with,
these days, any accapella has my dj on
the fade.
I don't believe in taking criticism, maybe
because I'm so far gone
Concluding my own habits, dreaming
of the future, in a life time.

I'll see settled if I live long, into the cycle under a sign,
Like a diamond in the sky forever practising in forms so fly
A little strength is all it takes to try, from the options of before,
Swinging wide, decide not to have belief in a lie. Afterwards.
The all time alibi, now is the time. Reasoning eventually the clue. Reality itself the tie, together is the usual way I get by.
Under the needle a tapestry manifests, unfolds, in multi coloured bloom.
Not unlike a laser beam bringing light into the room. If you can visualise this in your mind I'll then assume you have been told.
Cosmic mystic technicalities never too soon.
Cruel, so if anyone thought that I would loose it, another syllable will prove it, if I had a groove box I'd still be smooth.

Never ending strategy in a game like state has it's rules.
Not having to say that my emcee is hot when your ears are stuck like glue.
Altitudes like this have been around for years.
But in the beginning, only the foretold was old, the listeners had fears,
Inspired by their peers, rediscovering a resurgence in gears.
Selected knowledge collected, corrected, has always been near.
Taking advice, often, bettering my vibe on a secure ride.
Even if the plates slide, my God in a storm will decide carefully enlightening deeper pride.
Hear say has made me wild, it is no coincidence.
Never really closer to my childhood although you may believe this.
Intimidated writers wince when they learn of my existence.

Calmly calculated for my audience of course, since the last link substituted with a soulful wink.

I can often feel so good, when I'm motivated to explain as I should Systems so clever. Satisfying, qualified enrapture from the book.

Levelling bystanders minds you know that I would have to,

Introduce fresh endurance as I'd come to. Never fly through.

Superstitious to touch wood although my plastic scratches react.

Surfing tall, adding a delicate surface to the wall.

Until complete. This extreme of feats, designed still to greet,

La mode petit. The grand old fashion called discreet.

When you understand yourself, the heaven you create,

And with all that you know you'll have a reason then to play.

Working towards or away from every single day, even as you lay

263

If you find as you dream you pray, then your lover might say,
Life with the best of times and music has to stay.
Distinctive disintegration of paranoia in array.
It's just outstanding arrangement again
Waiting to find aggression so that I can inflict more pain,
I'm attacking in an insane way, since it's start, this procession.

Warning away the violence that came.
With confusion to blame released through the fortune of fame,
Reverence never plain. References to sin all just the same.

Always careful what I wish for, cause it usually becomes true
Naturally guided by above, it must be Love, I always knew.
Trustee of my own view so I'm concise tonight perpetually bright, instantly in sight, socially shrewd

Energy protective of it's nature in perspective of a mood, virtual adventure to me is food.

You've got to be aware that if I put you on a trip things may be different
Altered colours and sounds, a mysterious presence as if someone is around
People may seem strange, things you do preordained or even backwards.

They say it only happens on an 'e', but what's that meant to mean?
We cleared you and anyway you never even changed, it's just your brain
Arranging again just how you'd like to be, so follow me.

In a frenzied state of watchfulness, is it I'm granted? Wantant or wanted?
Take a trip into a poison mind with conspiracies that I have counted.

Reality over beauty of thought, another check you won't forget

Occasionally fashioned tempered steel shining bright, a shimmer
Against the rational I deliver, hardcore considered and then I let,
Radical people listen and sweat.

Two words, any two different words can hold a world, almost a universe of knowledge
Repeatable. I'm not sorry, cause I'm different, intricately honest.
What will come to be is what is. How existence though is justice.
Too many ways to touch this, admit it, it's busted.

The snowball effect, dreaming in puddles. Time.
Are we controlling them or are they controlling us?
My mind, in the future I trust, from my book of life, every line
Like pieces of a bomb, my knees are not weak, I am an expert.

With altering levels of communication of course as I start
A yin yang forever in process. You are everything and everything is you
Please note this interest, I've got some friends, and today I will phone up a few
Because I'm a man with news and I'm in deep interview so smart.
Polar explanation like the keys to a car, the blow behind the dart.

It's a present from me, a new programming strategy
If you need to know a safe step through for relaxation
Listen to me. It's no occasional secret that I keep
Freedom in bleeps, dance steps unique. Imagine art, imagine pressure both together. Nothing fresher!
Forget the previous lines of industry, I'm going to better.
A variety of device seen in films and pop video. Two little boys had two little

toys, they're mixing hip hop that you know.
Discovering a balance nominally on show, in display
As the music always says. Who am I to lie? I am on your side.
All around us so clear. If you know what I am thinking
It doesn't tell me not to try, here I describe through life in a vice,
Groove nature, my future's rhythmic desire, straight as your hi-fi.
As applied, with concern for effects and delayed, relayed learnt exponents.
Think twice, first for applicable, second for precise, the phase is even
The sky is the true teacher of meaning lined with stars at night.
Imagination burning bright, intellectual choosing of heavenly objects
Subject to throw light in beams to our arrays and yesterdays.

Something's going to change, I can tell things feel strange. Do I see hell?

What is going to happen? I know nobody would know
So I'm writing it down to examine what is shown.
Like a mystical vibe I see ripples in time again although not quite like before, now I'll explain.

We're all standing here, or over there, just like we might, tonight or on a different evening, everything it's clear, no fear.
Accepting this insight, most probably rhythmic definitely techno for the ear, so still specific,
In my mind are melodies almost self composed. Electric.
Directive, initiate the dancers thoughts with a language
Unspoken but polite on a level of divine light and sound.
The danger is apparent as I hear. Vocal quality possessed by me, of course my dream

Djs can follow me. If I leave you feeling scared just compare my manner to the clouds in the air.

Fear is what you need you will understand as living in this land takes it's toll upon your soul. I have catered and planned virtuous movement of the grandest.

Creations, crucial recollections in fact with these crescendos.

Shiny splendours and treasures to behold, now you're told, don't be forgetting, I ain't ever letting a lie to be bold.

As the message across the fader, never cold, hits the fold, becomes the crease, that which you and me see.

That hardcore sonic acoustic struggle finally making us free.

Settling the finest parts back in history, in touch with the industry commercial standards beckon peace to me.

Substantial to say, the stories from afar never old.

When I was young my mother would
scowl her little child.
Part of my learning, if I was wild, now in
her I can confide not that I ride, she'd
be so sad if I died
Then when I looked down from
Heaven my parents would cry.
Unending fly from the friends with the
attitude so dry. From mountainous
views down into valleys perceptions
slide
So who's on my side? Arrange to
profess and never hide.
No need to remember, from the vehicle
of time.
Only the initial coefficient plays, like an
abstract particle's existence,
The presence of a book full of words is
my ransom
You might think this is linked but
anyway finally portrayed are all the
rules to the game. It has a name.
Nightly beyond what I previously knew
to be as Love

Came the rush. You're so good, you remember enough of the case.
Why waste the slightest touch? We all chase what I prove to be the truth, but I'll still race.
Nightmares are set in a far off place, I still see your face
Just leave me alone and admit you submit, it's a trip. As I flick through the curses, made by lip, counted
My fellows dismounted, my ambitions dip. Answers arranged and equipped, nothing else ever so slick,
Come back to me, every other so quick, as my mind starts to settle.
This shelters unique, endlessly oblique, precious metals in an order so to speak.
I've acquired much practice, can you catch this? I understand this business
Always actually. In black magic I might have dabbled, only default
In direct association the substance catapults into another situation.
What are the convictions behind the way that you talk? Must remember

It is a method so tall, ballistics climb and fall, traditions crawl.

My crew fly, is there anything else? No, that is all. Forever sure description from a crystal ball

The finely tuned dj mind open to the headphones call.

Atmosphere obvious intelligence controlled in this haze

Natural ways. I'll apply as I see fly. Life's such a maze.

With my original style I am just careful, out to save other emcees, can't you tell checking is my thing for the rave.

Heart in it's place, mixing, is that fair? Create.

Movement and heat completely linked as the air I breathe

People's speaking weaves and I can't believe

I'm really so rude when I get across only what we really can trust.

No feeling ever crushed, even though I just touched what everybody does

In a complicated statement since what was is never looking back.
Filter fine attack stuck in the line of the track direct access all compact.
Taste the tactics in this non fiction act. Maybe I am the only one...
Sorting the worthwhile intensely logical I tally appropriately won. Now I cannot deny that I've begun. Exactly, this is only some.
If you were to study the way that time can stop, you'd only borrow,
Universal knowledge, sometimes a lot, how to be a crack plot. Read through confusing illusions or not, imagination blots But at last what you anticipate is this.
I am too quiet but you know the silent mind is never slow.
Be it your reality or friends around always reflecting the slightest glow
At least in expectancy when and if I talk it's going to flow.
So here's one for the mid range, two for the bass

And three to go. Compact ideas for our kind, superfluous in a state,
Blows across thought. From the beginning to the end, greater than naught.
Becoming what I am means that I am taught completely,
Sought after I wonder say the sounds I have caught.
In the sky again reversed and inverse signals and symbols.
This was never supposed to be a puzzle or mystery just to dissolve into what is equalled.
Ground breaking achievements and emotion proves
Independent foundation once loose, the start of the compound eventually news.

To be through music in my history, like a circuit of dreams.
Convincingly seen, I'll plan carefully, and as well as I can, out the team.

But I've become a weapon, the terminator, equaliser, moral pleaser, justice teaser,
Steadily quoted, notated for the sedated romancer, worldly wise dancer.
Golden rules of coincidence, number thirteen I am a chancer.
On hold is the information I may say, knowledge like a cancer.
Vinyl virtuality as prompt as you'd expect, static electric...
Perfected for any vicinity area or place, do you get a taste?
Connected to extra sensory perception runs the case through any bass.
Sixth sense, just a magnet like a semi precious stone for people with brains.
To life, fluid aims, digital games not naming names
I am still unattached, no ghouls or spectres are left anticipating what I have matched.
Beats of phonic measure, double turntable pleasure

Don't ever assume really what you are
thinking as the drums boom and the
intricacy of the tunes.
Forever onwards, upwards showing
closest to the truth.
This reliable scoop is on the move. Top
forty material any week
Musicians with the mission of babies
and peoples moods to sooth.

We don't need no grudges. If I was a
jackpot machine I would be full of
nudges,
A new found essence sludge's, slush's
across the clean floor creating a scene
Of security when all you need is the
new EP I'll have the definitive mixes and
break beats.
What is the difference between a dash
and a line? Does one take up more
time?
I like the fact that I follow other rapper's
rhyme, now you can follow mine.
The impossible constantly revealed
testing memory capacity like geometry.

Hesitantly wrought or ballistic simply well studied I can finish if all is fine.
I aim to drop as many comments as I can plausibly see, I'm instantly free
At first my practices were shaky, if I'm in reverse you may call it a fakie. Ike a printer I used to make mistakes, information miscalculated or misinterpreted.

X

On the breaker, good enough to feel watched but am I filmed? Untamed, underated?
Previous anonymous fame is my game. Next year, most things will stay the same way with equations although, much more to say.

Breathe and relay headstrong tales for some. I'm going to style so that this thing grows
Dropping jungle techno in a row.

The next volume I do not think will be the last because I own a past full of chaos,
My vinyl said save us in reality a myriad of tasks, some I surpass.
Feeling courageous as no bystander, my loops always track, black and white.
This is the plot no one ever forgot, what's bright is bright it's not a lot.
Are the ideas of the future so light hearted? It's what you've got.
Collectively should be deconstructed and considered the heart of natural entertainment.
I will trust that when you want to be amused it's unfair to be confused,
Thwarted or treated as children.
Everybody's equal in serendipitous surroundings.

All living in the same time is miracles
passage I am announcing. A control
surviving and dancing.
For a sensory output I have my mind
because how I feel,
Is my personality, life in a certain track
towards finality,
Touch future is back, all decisions
created inside the totally black.
In the gravity trap it's really you sliding
down into the gap
Forced to admit to any truthful pit of
space and time what it was
Functionally what it is. Illustrious,
obvious or lost in the mix.
It is every bodies moment, some have
tried, dedicated to the sun
Motions in colour, negative overcome
there is a meaning of life.

You always know who you're thinking
of, what and when because
No one need pretend that the data
flow will end, you are reality's friend.

Repetitive beats alone do not a pop
single make, it is the time that they take
Creating the perfect break, loops and
fades in the aim of trade
Copied, duplicated onto tapes,
whatever, or dub plates.

Super information, so I can build
systems that twist for this is what it is
In thought a key, the negative
respected premeditated spiritually in
angles set free
Reduced or so by me as I may teach,
show or coach the light I see coaxed.

For instance all I say or produce can be
doubled, the existence of quality is
manifold
Indisposed subjectively no trouble,
reconsider this air tight muddle.
No waiting from this under narrative
puzzler. I can get us there.

Angriest skies may seal our fate
although we exist to date. Latest
fashion icons on my list,
I still insist, are leading us all to this.
In the descriptive tense music sounds
most familiar to life.
It's first analogical explanations built up
often from the first note
Or initial beat. At a rhythm now is
driven a three hundred and sixty
Degree single motion of romance,
exhibiting existence of the past
Programmed computer functions may
preserve the reality but just dance.
Foot steps chosen in advance. I worked
it out because I had the chance.
Mild mannered I'll forgive, the lying
understood out of decency,
Represented in an album that now may
stay, compilation of array.
The huge gentle obeys providing views
of events at will
Spontaneously suggested if you're
listening closely enough until.

You realise yourself again, although you're not to blame, the force refills
And then fuels the second occurrence to be tamed
In completion is when knowledge of it's name will be gained.
Although some indents seem to never end, in a flurry of mysterious voices,
Only capable of worry, hurry through a toil of modern overkill replacing the same, jealousy is their game, colouring a spill.
This and that was how to scratch, how can you match? Fluid original technique which means much more than a keepsake.
I still of course like to challenge anyone who is able and available, to question this most tolerable of fables, noise sets the scene.
Sometimes, like right now I wonder how I can go on without a drum machine
It'd keep my feelings clean, for everyday as I've once spoken out schematics

Arranged about sinful influence
although yet I'll stay adherent to this
terminal
Hip hop advertisement coherent.
Show in full flow, sure master, head
ritual.
No bystander to such language will
ever understand, pacify experience
revealing grand
Forging rarities, reworking by hand to
beckoning philosopher's plans.
Gained again no motive but our charm
battling decisively past harm,
Complicated beyond elaborate choice
I've navigated a voice.
Original dispersion of instruments are
the dice.
So virtuous beat surrounding don't
drown, it's beauty assured,
Mystery measured, evidently self
tethered, propelled and bright
Here it comes across, what a realistic set
in sight.
Discovered that which controls us
makes us happy, why worry?

I was born to study, bodies of
symphonic architectural weight.
Arrived at a feeling imaginative may
migrate.

Check my drilling. My mind is porous,
your's is too, why start illing? Methods
here are filling all ways
I often pay the fare to adhere in my
dreams make other emcees scream at
the scene
Energies heard by my team, reflected
by the sky competitions multiply,
intensify growing ever fly.
Numero premier so turntable and vinyl
scare forever there, alternative
prospects are aware
The next dare leads me only to be able
to stare
If you can't read my mind you are
unlucky, I try to share.
Yes, I can be the best, everything
accomplished, why abolish?
Even remembering what was so funny,
so quick. Set essentially in itself is the link

How to do anything is written in my life time

I know that people who call themselves teacher don't want to admit mine.

Legislation more specific, every revision relentless, sonic tactics soak a new religion.

Coaxing incidental foundries so cool.

A mature druid wonders just where we're all from

It takes a mountain of mysteries observed to create some. Curved lines form from the spool introduced round how improved clear quoting smoothes.

Yin yang, destinies explosion, more hardcore proposals forever behind leading leaving forces described vocal.

A little lyrical confession at provision I now apply,

Further rhythmic tantalisation from a guy with the sky in his eyes,

Fresher tactics than yours? You surprise me. Here's some words,

That you can add to the force and so endorse one

Even my dreams are fun so don't waste
your time with hate.
Or suspicious, malicious confusion like a
teenagers youth here's appropriate
determined proof.

Love makes the world go round, it is
written in a book and another and
another book, energies cook
The groove aware has took. Sometimes
I'm alone
It might be the way I look, resistant
together, hardcore is forever.
On the edge of what we all have still
happening as it should.
Hyper exposure in global mass media I
desire intelligent fires, considerable
highs answer any why.
Particles positive for atoms, when will
anyone notice.
The course of nature is God, once
upon a time when man was primitive
This was thought of as odd with no
sixth sense dictating

Power of words usually rewarding
generating sympathy appraisal.
When thousands of years later, sense is
vital, jungles are tamed,
Top classes are blamed, encyclopaedic
knowledge, the information train.
When I think or look back I mustn't
worry, over my history I hurry.
Certain bionic principles are new, eerie
disposable views. Last night, my darling,
I was invisible. The latest scribble
Complete in two colours, arranging the
invincible style, understood at least by
other hip hop fellows is left to mellow,
So we can tomorrow acknowledge
carefully recognised sorrow.
Independent basslines bellow relaying
what follows.
Caution as applicable as fun, here to be
experienced by some
Most of my learned friends will
convince me that it's begun.
Reality evolution, racialist powers add
up and multiply hour by hour

With standing is my occupance of space by time devoured.
Another alternative vie, any facing me
It is after you and me. Only or all, yourself.
So it's alive proportionately, not knowing what has started.
No one could dream, options are available. Why wreck anyone?
You are becoming itself, beckoning index of reflex, you know it's begun.
Future feature, cool core. Multi core groove equipped clip, creation of the lines.
The knife removed is a struggle, the answers in a race condition, objectives in selected statistics, tactfully only are there two sides to politics
Since nineteen ninety three played bionics and stories, even films of ruin.
Cultural natural, I'll break the bonds echoing on
Any second that I choose can be my history that I've evolved from

Earlier recollections succumb, the sound is numb
Altered this dimension and frequency saved by some.
Don't do it, don't say it
Everyone's the same, can we get a contest?
On a silver computer gold is a super snooper
In crest. Don't live in black and white.
Someday we'll get it right.
Neutrons revolving
Man's obviously solving. Astral codes
Lesser nodes, do we do the same?
Easy new ideas, a pure side,
constructed to retain.
Rippled angles in the sky and in the rain
What if when it started anything could be plain
However long ago, crescendos remain in your frame
With still possibly the future to blame.
The colour of life I would name,
enhanced draught

Of selective insight merely arranged right, diagnostic out of sight.

I thought that you liked me, we were bad
And now and again I can't get you out of my mind, am I mad?
Being apart from you is just sad. It can take so much energy
As you ghost. Memories coast, emcees boast.
No one will ever turn back time
Now you know that once you were mine.
It is easy to see you are so wrong about me, being unkind
Originally in my sleep I find craft the legacies that blind.
So much space between us defines the rewind.
Firstly, all the passive quotation I mention is forever devoid of hateful intentions.

Second, accuracy here could win a prize, why confuse yourself with my rise?

Cause and effect, moments to decide, fast as machine gun fire.

Solid objects, desire, animations slide amongst two sides

Or more. Insanity suggests the end, completeness, a ride.

It's just for once I could say, you put words in my mind.

How far can it go? I don't know. Now you are not so blind.

Life for me should be easier, no one would ever care.

But I can really be better over time that we share.

And images, sights, sounds, feelings and thoughts

Altogether true, forever there.

Want and hate, two watch words for the steady but bright,

No revenge makes compensation in charge of what's in light.

Balance, poetic justice is how I like to play
Bringing forth like a laser beam the next way.
Capital images of everyday to hold onto as I sway.
Convincing the them to get out of it again.
Easy as a compact disc, mothers and teachers will be with this
Over active connection with relative state of bliss.
Getting over decisions like a formula mechanic the sky insists
Staying easily understood are the visions that come with this acoustic kiss.
Outgrowing unfair tactics, I am a better breed in pact.
Can you tell? What I learnt in this country nearly hurt me, hell!
I should call myself something good, quicker although true
You'll wish your parents never knew, just what you do in fact.

293

It doesn't matter what day it is, I'm happy to be working,
Concentrating hard then resting, connecting matters to a cause.
Super chemicals are yours. I'm not the boss although I manage my position
As if kids could be listening to this standard I'm revisiting.
Nuclear conclusion to unclear education are politic's pathway
Like your game and it's scart lead, another information seed.

If I didn't believe I'd swear things would breakdown
In my habitat, for God's sake, what is tripping?
Worry, but honour. If I can take your pain away I'll just borrow
How it feels to know unachieved goals. Slightly misplaced fools,
Irrelevant tools grow from a transparent garden such affirmative soils.
Planet Earth, is it the beast? Or all are we clean? Life is the machine

Dreams are a chill, water vapour in a pill, the seed is sown. Deteriorating never is the now obvious overkill blown.

Getting into the mind it is OK, on my own the evil is shown

Or other dumb forces meaninglessly blown away

Dust to dust, dusk 'til dawn, double plus love from up above.

Here comes a glove, so that an army in the jungle can be born.

Secluded morals don't exist, I own my hits. Knowing how to check them

Vibes persist, insist that I choose the right things to say,

Even clearer today texting in the mix. The past I leave behind obviously not good enough for me

Individually unscared, unamused, unmoved. How could I trade?

Voices of those I now know to be full of evil

Bass waits in every place, my mind makes you all equal.

My lifetime, synthetic rays consume my space
Why is this a dream war? Six hundred and eighty reasons
Not to swear or play not knowing.
How to go on, on my own a final reason I should not forget.
Creating sounds to translate, pictures of fate shine
From mind to mind specifically remind, prayers for reality,
Clarity never wanting to undo, the free time's all for me.
I don't want to cause any pain in any individual it's plain.
Collecting again loves as which I've never known.
Coming again, playing with the sharps never condoned.
I own the tone of serious suggestion here that I like, and I wonder
If you have always wanted to just feel what you want,

In my own eyes it is only true. Attitudes built from what you knew. Experience, predominating performance on offer.
Still people hardly would notice one another
Without being mentioned, the reality from this brother.
Executed are all that matters, at all to ourselves
Within our health, never without the time or life's wealth.
Operating averagely, out to find number one
Manners are charming, ecstasy only harming the balance of age.
As I read the next page an energy is saved.
Lights follow rhythm which comes from within a gauge.
Independent, focused and willing, I like to leave the competitors chilling.
I could be filling your desires, satisfaction and relief. Belief in human nature, as it takes a vibe to remove your grief.

Djs might as well admit we see straight through
Something even if it is legit. Sex is creation!
Occasionally my speedy narration will dive a bit.
Here's the suggested grip, time changing colours, then I quit.
Why are you here? What is the meaning of life if it keeps us alive?
Put here by a stronger force in need for decryption that I have seen.
That is to say, refuse and methods become refuge, solitude in pain
Wildest studies and attributes turning around. Remember vein?
Whoever said that God and drugs don't work? Reality is bezerk.
I know that you've had insight in occasional bursts,
Occult figures may really observe while leaders deserve.
Oxygen challenging words. Scratches on a CD like the wind.

I am aware that someone will possess
my brilliance,
For my audience I choose, steadily
amusing rules.
Inspired by Elvis, once more maintained
are schedules he'd not agree with
Here I have to share my station
modularly.
How to make successful records,
hopefully charting
There will always be flavours for those
unquestionable sales.
Ballistic remedies to home truths, for
anyone in their youth
And as we're older still maintaining a
truth in it's proof form.
The social jungle warms. Three to four
minutes in a storm
Coincidently recognised fantasies are
born. In a will.
Commercial production oversees and
chills.
Words and tones, naff design
overthrown, wages are blown.

Money for convenience, money for the music maker.
To infinity the singles market is a world wide player, stayer, religion slayer, automatic sayer, financial portrayer.
Systems morph, hardly a benefit this genius clause, mixing a reality amidst a class war.

Jacobs ladder Earth from early signs of breaks in the plates,
So far although maybe just explored.
What is a planet's weight?
Left only eternal the correct justice and fate of the perfect distances
Harmony will only ever bring across a galaxy life, does the beat go on?
Religion claims, puts an answer to maybe what you don't know
Although you don't know, you could, cause it does show.
Every single day maybe tricks in my ears could frighten me
Conception, liability the possibilities in this world are tremendous.

This solar neat fashion conscious
collector of lives often rebellious,
Orbitally written, as gods given facility,
so life has persuasion
Seriousness, attitudes in grace for trade.
How have you got it made?
You should know you're the centre of
the universe as human feelings
For hundreds of decades. Sorry to tell
you now that we could be on the
Way back, forces on track when you
find out what you really shouldn't.
And futures attack, time escalates at
impact only, with no gap.
Common issues are just lapse
compared in a fear level noted.
Castling imperial realistics for voted,
interestingly posted, I bet that
You believe there's been a war, don't
get out dated, belated
Bizarrely modulated, two hundred
times ten, everything around again
Don't do it and you could be saved,
wicked times can be said the same as
prayers.

Heaven's stairs, does anybody learn to share? Love this care.

Everything mostly including the whole wide world part of the mystery there.

Anytime we still should wonder how it started and how to escape

Realities gape, incredible vapours, is it just a sound? Around since created

Very forcefully holding us together ignited, the disassembled things

Still borrowed and resourceful it sings. Belief in a sting

I never pretend virtue of God, settling what is odd in a mood swing.

This here emcee's still alone, seems like a good idea through time but everybody needs a real Love to get by

Once so near, viciously severe, nowadays my head is never clear.

Introductive values are for sale, life has left me pale. Interactive dreams let me see you fly, as you are

Expand my consciousness while I'm asleep over distances of far.

Why does it get like this, watched through the mist?
If I'd have stuck to an evil game, who would be the same?
Though eventually it'll drain a force, a steep coincidental
Happy to change because I can, the way of my name. Still situations in my brain sequent the insane
For frequencies plain. Jam home selector the pain. Exchanging trades for skin as the reverb begins.
Sketching down my event horizons could be monumental to my father
So encouraging, the fundamentals of existence I will achieve through chance. You I will slay
Because time has had it's play, I'm the only one with the memory to say.
Dark images float around, decay as in the shadow all may. Treasured that which stays. Placid unaffray.

Thanks, so often I've been distracted by it. Chemical association only your fault. Why disqualify?

Understanding of such levels and formats are here clear,

Never dismissing, only tackling the extreme severe. Twister of logic, but systems really I show

Readily rechallenging bystanders on a low. My mind realistically glows, remembering a heat,

Happier with you as I check out any beat. Last week was ridiculous. Furious heads may meet

Respect for what is neat in an order so far complete.

Since birth your eternal spirit has been captured in a soul, taken away from reality to become a whole.

From Heaven unto nature, life's effervescent vapour.

As you know. All that they understand maybe this, accelerating culture.

Continuing with problems that I've had since I was young. Minor attachments defining what is sung.
Ever since my early interest in anything, came along the subject
Of misuse, appropriate but opposite views. Mix and contrast,
Newest machine code fast designed, as an attractor. Filter and scratch,
Persistent catches, life's third element in a snatch.
Release of my knowledge forms a mainframe so honest
Existing collaborative mentioned is the toughest if one could measure courage.
Arranged into a scale we will flourish behind and through resistance
Collectively mindful past a punishing distance concealed.
Concentration in perception building on a deal eventually settling free beyond real.

Lighting conditions for finer issues to see anger from any heart aligned unto thee.

Teachers, astronomers, preachers and astronauts
Waiting to be granted areas of logic so dumbfounded. Surrounded all this time in doubt. Exactly what the expanding universe is about. Never discussing leaving to whenever the discoverer's trust.

Some hope for no more suffering yet advancements must cause
Rearranged angles from a courtyard of nature, a crust.
Documented here forever lies. The key most dormant.
As such only rhythms buzz, only time decays, the clash cuts the dream.
The parts I only made to be presented to you
Mean nothing but they have to persuade.

Solutionists, nationalists, workers and
soldiers
None of whom realised until they were
older. Life's immortal game.
Cruel, relentless sources they overcame,
nominal winnings are narrow.
From the unlikely to follow,
indiscriminately unravelled.
Started by you unless, you are
dreaming. Only happening and new
Frontline scores contain the meaning
straight through.

True it is I the only one with the
combination. Any particle reveals this
Latin formulation
To noone, at no times sending
witnesses blind mad, stimulants and
man has.

Basis and rhythm through which you
call reality tears, they don't know the
meanings of time, they are scales,

Monoliths of tales, objects diverting such failings beside that jading exposure of something never found.
Acuteness amounts to insurance in trails
Reasons respond and pound, familiar movements through the crowds.
Back across loud terrain I am proud of sound clean, continuation we are down for.
Transverse occupying a void of secret G force in the place
Let it rest but not waste in any degree of disgrace.

I was left in a program, no fault of my own, just like the last thief.
Who and why anyone would condemn me in the zone I don't really know.
It starts a new belief or more in Heaven, life, virtuality.
True death scares me, why is my history full of such variants?

I watch the law, check the score
everyday in the paper
But what do these chevrons mean? Do
people believe in television?
What they say, crazier whole new ways
like sexy visions, if this don't threaten
me, would I still act?
Enabling fact, devoted vicious
reasonings attract.
L.P. license phenomenon, L.P. license
phenomenon,
I've been around for an eon, a
millennium or two or a century.
The year of the dragon hold mysteries
still for these hip hop hearts.
Don't break, honoured in tradition
mirror images at stake.
Witnessing revolution begin for the
light of our skies, the natural
adaptations trail, only the best survive
Merging feelings converge and fly on
and on. Energy in every structure like a
song.

Twenty two gasps of pleasure in
between, rolling, examining parts that
I'm holding
With growing concern for the cold air
that is blowing.
Showing that the history I'm towing is a
scene. To the sky when anybody's
clever and wise
Seen same as yesterday, we formulate
and survive learning new things that
you have never tried.
My thoughts do not dwell on negativity
like hate, disgrace or shame, only again
From a state of fortune in a parallel fate
to blame.

XI

Ceasing mixing up records that I could
be releasing

My manner meaninglessly vain just like
the automatic super highway train.
Practised and rehearsed through
complicated ways.
Participating in mysterious ways and
fades that we all create trading the far
out as fair as I can say.

You've always been interested in design
jealousy counterbalanced,
And getting us over advances in such
technology as it arises,
Advice, moral fibre, brittle like ice ,
summarises the real challenge.
Misplaced trust down to unclear cries,
Part of the unseen crisis, narrow
modern life confirms this.
Who deserves this? A percentage of
side line customers refine this.
It's nice to rely on when no one's mind
is quizzed, the interpreted version
structured against decay.
Population's way. No one thing that
anybody could say will slide,

Get on a good ride. Beckon time until it
glides away.
Subjects slowly will obey, just like they
really did yesterday. A heartbeat
coincides with all decisions made.

Lyrics are assuming the method is in
what is soothing.
Moving down through the list of
enabled pieces of time,
Now surer than ever that this
knowledge is mine.
A magnet of ariel symmetrics to be
heard so fast forward or in reverse
observe.
Life could be a lotion, you're all only
yourselves in perpetual motion, unto
death,
Never easy with roots in history which
can only be left.
Karma threatens peace which ain't at
this moment in release
Born into the prison of the mind until
the reasons cease.

Children in a revolution don't notice
although grow up and believe
Every day driving the devil onwards to
plague and tease.
Some realise these were the days, and
still are, with beats...

You never told me that you are psychic,
I see you moving from afar
And even in the rain you are vague,
vain and translucent.
Introduce me to agreement that we
start. I am the yin yang, the wheels of
the motor car.
Also into vital translations from
observations, deciphered my way
Arrangements stay, bookmakers are
paid while compact disc plays.
Who believes in the new gene or
nature's spring clean?
Jump behind the control stick of this
flying machine.
"If you're going to pretend that you
don't care don't look up."

All around the dub will surround any air seeming corrupt.

Discontinued now are taunts which you may want

Doubling what you thought wouldn't even when you don't.

Critically acclaimed remembered and renumbered frame by frame. Long live the game!

Tips of time going nowhere frees the beat, the beginning indicator a relief

Suggestions in retail belief, supposed coincidence because what is followed now sweet.

First definitive meanings oxidise reacting like sound as big and as loud as you feel.

Around the structure lies boundaries and passages innocently found. Don't ever feel careless or blameless as this period is explored.

Underground, the only way it ever works, artificial intelligence here for you and me, bezerk it pounds.

Such quirks only together will survive, in only complete function,

Wholly will ever exist, from my mind to yours so admit. I am down.

I think you know that it does, everyone should.

More than I see now, people in the future will look back

And say, whatever happened to yesterday?

Everything's still here but how did it stay?

There are questions on everybody's lips evolving that shouldn't exist,

That will leave the human race in a pit.

Able to admit, the story must change, finally I have learnt

More versatile than I thought, now so much interaction is

Control in the area, raced, forced and searched

For what's never been before, I'm back again with hardcore.

Worry about yourself, learn to even see yourself!

Because all you deal with are intentions
from the next dimension
Growing up is hard to do especially for
children facing what is new
In the schools learning reality while the
quality of rules affects the few.
The hip hop idea, who is winning? I've
got a style that is never diminishing.
Termination rights and end license
agreements, how can I make this up?
Watch the cuts, choose the force, white
noise, and a Porsche.
I also like Ferrari and the way that the
team scores. What would it take? A
sampler, a T.V. screen, digital
harmonics, a laser beam.
Convincing concerned alliances to
dream. More technology and less work
will make me faster,
It's no disaster, no coincidence, just
mental applied resistance, I am a
master.
Information technically assisted. I am a
dj so I do what the hell I like

Writing the rhythm almost every night catch twenty two is not how I choose to be gifted.

Trying to escape as I admit this through the morphing music business.

Rolling, hypothetically twisted, God wished for this

And of course it comes true. So now what can we do? Premeditated genius gathers force waiting for the time,

When the rest of hardcore will explicitly reign. Since a fiery sign in the sky manifests plain.

Democracy emergency. Emcees make the b boys days, left so sharp to say.

It is so harmless, married to a time and only even wanting to mix,

Socialise, I have got to tell you this. I've been in practice for years

Since sixteen, dealing with playing out, developing faith.

Meeting each other, once in the past there existed but one doubt. Patronage, misled compulsions reveal how it is with no change.

Dire searchless narration obtained in a physical lift. Darker than life riffs, valleys still hidden by still.

As we age, moral depictions are strange and always about.

I've vowed I'll be incharge with myself for clarity

Alarmed by the rate of mismanagement in deities all wound up.

I still don't understand, why the cover up?

Who knows what exactly is corrupt.

Only expand, E equals emcee squared, argue.

Everyone sharing the quantum physics that we became from

Colossal hemispheres and the new valleys of Love,

As perfectly as ever, so precise as is written, signed by the above. Initiative inductees repairing repeated remarks and newer symbolic considerations fulfilling solely beauty of

Geographical quarks, historical arks and other landmarks.
I've always tried my best, not to break my neck, when I'm containing higher feelings for past treks.
As my paralysed mind wonders what's next, gravity keeps my soul earthed to the decks.
Erogenous conclusion. A focused, hidden harmonising sweat.
Exclamation replaced with better words, for better verse.
Riding sense lets continuation burst, since the very first. Melted association in sight, too bright
Radio phonics are the key to life, day or night, stereo polyphonic insight in trade for politics.
Just so nice! Changing subject matter to the extra, I am such a serious selector.
Looking at the world, listening to the sound of now,
Currently working on the film of how I've been so let down.

Written myself out over ten times already.

Tripping like I've finished the design of the finest, finally no doubt. Ripping, insanity for sale guaranteed not to last has been about.

Lectures run on and on, law only touches devout.

I take little notice even of what I believe because it's hardcore.

Politically on trust from God or another time lord,

Agencies respond in haste, to solve the space and accord, Whatever they can afford invested in the word.

In this job you've got to be qualified, adaptable

Amplifiable in your tone of mind, never deaf dumb or blind.

Free senses chill, in a language of attitude and skill. True complete ability that can kill, arranged at will.

Merges, stages, phases in balance are still, Harmonic distortion is only your mind and it's seal.

Believe. For real.

It's new, parallel patterns on cue, the fabled fade able view.

Forever cute bionic mute moves from the tune skater.

Narrowing, trimming and all cut up, is the rough abrupt style.

And mood slater. Deceiving the moon for a while until later,

I believe that the music that you hear could not be greater,

So easy to find a rhythm and relation in the natural equation. Mindful salvation.

And now how simple it is to understand,

Hell just a place made up by people for people who are bad.

Life is the reality of sound mostly to me

Whenever you are down there will always be vision in your mind or in your eyes.

Existence seems so stable because we expect it to be, in choice

Realise that your voice is the extension
of possibility in noise.
Freedom of frequency bands in verse,
never worse. Occasionally even your
pleasures will reverse, it's no curse.
I am trying to work out why I am
confused again,
Feeling blue once more, versions of
answers are new and raw.
To you and I personally I have sided
before trying obviously to contain
which is more.
Near genius explanation to the letter of
which is better.
Confidence so highly held, no sweat
although a swelter.
Anytime, and then in reference easy
rhythm settlers,
To my home boys I always kick out the
first thing on my mind
It is never uncool. Upgrading in
software and recording facilities
Flashbacks and nightmares if I fall
asleep on these. Reversals, transitions,
dictations versus how I breathe, see

and believe. Contagious diseases are like a curse to me.

Medicine I just don't understand, so release the trigger and pitch the gate Complete consequential answer to your fate.
Voodoo operations just too late. Vivid in a source. Graduating
Related by the words I sow the credits like seeds.
Time curves. Theories are sweet, narrow ideas coming to light. Advertise the fight, sell out hidden pros.

People needn't think I'm down because I think, it's when I've caught up with you I need a drink.
Purists on their own side searching for a link, catch the virtual blink, oversee the brink.
You got to know it's true when the words are straight from a dream factory.

I've won. Game, set and match. Which is why exactly you were worried.
I still hurry, for where I am, in centre of gravity I am not heavy. My deity is now collated history.
I'm blistering. Correctly, exactly an attack.
A ruthless identity battle through x amount of matters I may back.
Marked territory exposed in refreshing gaps, interesting by lines in a flash. Such a snap.
Moral adjustment is rap! Coded poetic parts in a sharp.

Evaluation of content in your heart. Straight with the force like a dart.
An arrow, moves across with symmetry left alone as one symphony.

To say is as bad to hear, so I'll leave rappers in fear of the truth. One hundred percent proof,
Blood is the key. Gravity. But how can you tell I'm sincere? I fly over every

groove with the un dying Levels to choose. Criticism of my operation will confuse no useless melody behind which simultaneously Reviewed. Although sometimes I don't understand, I just try to make sense somewhere before I die.

Fashioned by the ones who want to hate us, or fate us, disrupting a course, disrupting of course.
Watched by primeval eyes depicting, afflicting, re corrupting innocence commonly addictive.

Cycling of metaphors reform a state, molecules and atoms relate to actual dates
Beyond a physical ambience heard only too late reconsidered by me to narrate.
Natural hi-fi, indigenous to this species as we know might even grow on undiscovered planets

In various groves. In unseen jungles on show. Back to basics is this undercover nitro.

Working, earner, decider, learner.

Once before I left it in the middle, I was easily catching up

Like a footballer with the dribble to the hip hop fiddle.

I never wanted to be un accurate in my mission as I try to take note on every single collision.

Widely varying degrees of contact to my brain cells re enacting just what ravers dispel,

Repelling like a hired gun in contract, opponents fell

From hearing the unlicensed rhyme that I'd learnt well.

History of my art, part three, still managing to breathe

As my blood flows as rivers to the sea, coordinated decisively,

Ripped apart an -ology, from a dogmatic start as a younger seed

Considered by all to reflect no greed. I
don't inhibit the scene, still maintain
higher quality to believe
Cutting every rhythm so clean that rivals
feared I'm a machine. Blur if I move too
fast in the night club,
Separating the hot from the cold in this
war of Love. Double-dutch driving the
darkest in dub. Intelligent lectures as
always a message from above.
Coincidental rumours at a touch, my
nemesis of trust. Does well to lyrically
bust and manage what it must. Two
evenings later, I set the alarm and wait
nocturnally like dust.
Stop me if I scare you, or tell you
something old that you're already
aware of.
I don't quite know how to go from
here or how far just because.
Reality beckons, though loops and the
force rolls.
Never ever stole other people's break
beats although I note how they
corrode.

Still now I am still in stasis, familiar
haunts but I'm no prisoner to these
places,
My mind expands or doubles up
because of various hot rappers on that I
base this.
Records revolve and I solve play lists,
what I need, lots of space to console
hits.
In the dark I'll be blacker, with lights on
the mixer and my soul in the track,
Words gets round of the art I am
another cracker. Bassline attractor,
Digital convenience inter actor,
intermediately in pact.
I've been playing your records since I
started mixing tunes,
Many years ago on the two quartz lock
I can move.
I had to give it up because it cost more
money than sense
Then the revolution would commence.
I've got a stance.
Plus so many questions to ask, is this
supposed to clear and close.

The entire subject and all reliefs? Or add up to the flow of nouveau.
Recite and remind yourself what is right. Follow my solo.
In any order I will continue to recommend in any tense, narrow virtuoso.
Invisible people around me laugh, I don't mind ghosts they're stuck in their paths.
Supernatural some call the other side, indivisible substance to the last.
Letters in a formula propel matters as clear and as fast
Stay away from hell, believe in what you tell, life becomes the past.
Deeds multiplied by a half, designed to sell.
Intent on any new vibe, develop and blast.
Never cutting corners with rhythm on a mission
Decision on the focus then realism.
Solely terminal decisions, followed swiftly like a standard or class.

Mathematics can sometimes be difficult, like coming to terms, politics or an insult.

Re collectively should I start or give up my career? I never got any nearer,

Some men and women understand this style, and then some don't. Don't feel threatened by my reflections, they are no front.

Old friends just disappear, clearer skies actually worth money, cash, dollar

I'll follow although I won't curse, unless I need to return on the first.

Through many cycles still rehearsing for the sake of a fresh burst.

Through sorrow pressure repeats, un consequential I remember before tomorrow.

I've lost sleep, regained dismembered bleeps. I keep my loops, retain hope

Because I concentrate and remember every note, from my past times I quote,

Passed lines, hot rhymes, formulised stunts and skills I mill.

I do not control everybody that I see although they are captive in the same beat.
New software for notation and grooves, life on the move we positively prove.
Keep on top, keeping in the track, supersonic kaleidoscope.
When the patterns converge the images stay landscape or portrait
Universally to this day, on my head I'll adopt this and never loose.
When society gets jealous just mellow. I heard it on the news.

XII

Pick my subject matter up and put it down again, from the beginning, forever chilling.

In a different place I state a case remaining willing, aging gaps diminishing.
Detail coded in itself, unfinished explanation, aqua sonic equations in relation.
I will fold any fear, dry the last tear, drop behind the horizon listening to the feeling.
Followings believing realistic intentions from the heart close from the start, apart.
Discovering your deeper styles like stars. I'll fall, arranged pieces call.
And they pounced, negative issues to the ounce, I clean my feet, brush my teeth, while others sleep.
Then I win from the margin steadily proposing what I'll keep.
Acoustic announcement in charge draining the bounce from the deep.
Intimately reclusive the new time is a story in response. So I'll proceed with my exclusive shading style that sweeps,

At once a freedom steeps and recollections creep.
To the cold winds carrying obsessed souls
Because the rhyme don't lie I'm showing you what's been told.
In the heart of the weather several promises turn to gold
Mechanisms re shape to their justice manifold.
Answers on a plate, from the sky, shining like stars far and wide,
Rendezvous to the chariots of old.
Coming again the wind it blows.
I don't know what's going on in a game of constant illusion,
Hearing a different song, singing surges into instant solutions.
Maximum peace to my past, and passed laughs. Great tasks, shaded and masked designer of facts,
Basic and always subtle, intimate cracks, following intermediate shuffles that I back.

As I once again find what disturbs me
in my mind I am free, I can be just what
I want, if I try.

Pay for it now or later just got to relate
to the rapture reprising
Don't ever take away, create! Flashback
in a heaven's eye.
Under estimated every day in life.
Analysed all that glitters,
Gold and silver in delicate intricacy.
Measured, listed,
Punctuated with fine nature in air of
surveillance first. Ballistic
Coincidental textures adding matter as
insisted.
Remarkably conflicting energy co
existed in a parallel plain, pleads fall on
vain ears, besides another game. Finger
tip control tweaks the metal, the final
settle?
Basslines double and the rhythm
trebles.

Tonight the nightmares are only on TV,
bubbles relax to the rhythmic beat,
Every heart endlessly in sync with deep
thought, after a pause... reality
New excuses in art, dots and codes,
replacing the moral mode.
Over the time spent obscurely showed
virtual cartoon, cartoons in a row.
Under regulated or the law, the
techniques I saw roll, everybody's
favourite features
Testing repeated episodes and issues,
directed flavours from the soul.
Onward unthwarted flow dominating
specialist areas of interest in a zone
Forward into every reflection that is
known. Your cover is blown.

I can trust you because we met on the
same ground, working together in
sound
Communication in at last believable in
frequencies pitched down. Some dj
invented this method of all techniques,
let it be found.

Sitting in class again, not sure whether to listen to the drone, I'm prone.
It is better to think for myself. Living signs sing unknown.
Caressing the chrome, identical reasons can be left alone.

Combat drill so adequately named.
Before it's time some say,
Relentless attitude for permanent ways discovering what is still.
Achievements of the will recorded in black.
Very luckily blessed, my own tests are mostly archived as fact.
So don't be vexed, you'll wonder how it is possible, how it all connects
But forwards, backwards, inside out it's the best and it's large, in effect.

Process one, initialisation. Every bone in my body cracks
In serialisation the explanation is back.
Free style layouts will attack.

No red ink, as just what is said is what I
think. Mental will.
Contagious rapture in spill. When the
lion awakes, reality will fill.
Waiting for the world to mix up so I can
show my skill, until
The forces that want control, find a
way, relentlessly chill.
Magic evil is not the way of the sequel,
keep buying
Ambience for your life that is
enlightening and peaceful.
What can I tell you, staying up all night
writing something to sell you.
Am I ill or is it public demand. Bettering
standard, minimizing wonder,
Nature yells. Assume, renumber. It'll
only sound like how you make it sing.
Concrete facts are clues for the few, as
are the beauty that they may bring.
The air insists that I exist, the skies tell
what I've done, exposed on the run
Special effects just for who it affects,
every time on the line, the expansion
begun.

Alternate colours lift from above forming to the sun in view, the groove is one.
Past moves from a list include a compound reaction that's hard to improve.
Double Love is always high like a candle, I don't know why, Love flies Easily like a jet or at the speed of light on the internet, vibes collide.
Enveloped as if in some kind of ride. My routine allows the brain to decide This overture of power of course cannot hide.
I know that you want to start with the 't' but you can't when you follow me. Breaking the lines every time. Super rhyme.
Panoramic guns on tracks will intervene as if you need an explanation.
Distortion in time causes panic and I have the solution.
Soldiers on cross faders analysing the pollution, adopting the want.

Because once someone actually caught up with me it burns
Spoken are some, unforgotten is the count. My stunt warns as it warms,
Chills as it performs, puts you in a spell, disappears in a form.
Arguments are born, expectations a charm, magnify from afar.
Dislocating tones. Vocal scars are torn like the stars in the sky of time.
Digital finds for the eye of the mind. The un ending situation.
Every frame is only what you're ready for. Before I really knew you,
I estimated any single mind, every golden find, any bionic kind.
In unity we deliberate, friends around just do gyrate.
Any massive bass navigate, all dance steps quick to coordinate.
Chilling in the scene forever killing, I'm willing.
Let the people dance, jump up and touch the ceiling,

Bodies that can't keep up, disrupt and
I'm so feeling
Nothing ever goes wrong while we're
believing.

In the screen, I believe to be adopting
clean shades of youth
Moving through energies consistent
with proof, engines of the day,
Alchemy in the way, listen to what I say
Revenge is a method in my name, same
as yesterday.
What can I do if I Love you? Helping
you out, in the pure
Rush towards unending excitement
how you always knew and pretend. It is
just torture. Running without you in
nurture
Comprehend the buyer's end for the
third time publicly sent.
You know you're only on a clue now so
you shouldn't care if in outer space
you're still a case,

Two thousand and gone and still looking for dinosaurs to grill from their face.
Living beside a pill or a trip, recover in days.
Reanalyse over years, bad things in my life disappear.
Together clever verse become law, I adore.

There is a tangent though, arranged bestowed, to have known. Dedicated arrangements shown alone, the clone of a clone.
Again is the wonderland scene of machines in a dream. Exotic electro in static regime.
Really pushing pressure up, gravity down.
Found through boundless dates all around,
Standing for a sound, or new ground.
Owners of this virtual reality are renowned.

Talent allowed, transactionally relative issues cloud, heavy weight accomplishment until the future drowns.
Distinction bound. It is so nice, I can slice,
Wicked mix tunes in the middle of the night.
All day, rain or shine facing a positive structure that is mine.

Why I ain't writing, it's frightening.
Enlightening essays from me, ending with a please, I'm reconciling.
Compiling built up data in all ways.
Still breaking. Correcting, shaking foundation,
working the crowd into a trance.
Occupation in advance, the bassline attracted to the dance. Overseen by chance.
This is what you want, when everything you need is in front. I am in control, you can touch what was once.
She is lost, I have no doubt of the cost.

342

Beats reminding of a day, infinitely improbable but still the way to stay. Showing the paths that even you could obey.
Digital translucence for everyone, everyday.
Spearhead of information in delay.
Cut up are the pieces that we say, come what may.
Computer graphics in his youth,
I don't understand this gangsters proof.
Anyone can see the inside of this sanctuary,
It left a history and a story that is legendary.
A sealed beast had been in containment for a long time.
Following this rhyme, binding what is done,
You are believing in a blinding light from above. An ice cold symmetry, winding matters pass in love.
Perfection in a scent, corny World wide patronage, Absolution through a vent, success is what I meant.

Rapping like this from the Heart
Leaves me with a dent and the glory,
Any other open minded story is what
you'll choose.
Who doesn't play gravity and ride on
time?
A compact disc means beats all the
while.
Living on the side, opposites attract,
worlds collide, left with nothing to
achieve but slide? Never realise
On vinyl scriptures and metaphors are
high,
resounding a diamond. Mounting
evidence to decide, or accordingly on
video tape,
nothing like this can be captured, just
try it, create.
Identical tunes are the closest it gets to
Heaven. You've got to wait.
Anything can be done these days with
computer graphics. Newly realistic
breathing in digital habits.
All men are created equal in a way.

Creation is at bay. Latest technology is bought
then it decays, over and over again,
The actual craze relays.
Gone are previous feelings towards maybe the whole planet,
Under used emotions in the Universe will jam it.
Everybody in the innocent internet collective, dynamic.
Dusted trusted double existence causes trouble in another land.
Understanding the largest of mysteries had never been planned.
Settling coincidence is science, making fiction a fact
Trend setting logistics tangling tomorrow
come back.

I can't write that fast, so I had an idea, that has got to be flexible,
Feeling really scared when I am heard, makes me want to attack.
I am learning the magic in reality,

it just about works with no catch.
Still got to act. Invincible undetectable without
an ion won't put me off.
Reliance relays, iron Zion tops.
If you can't mirror this drop.
My emcees will never stop. Living in electric shock.
The clue is in speech or all talk,
splitting as I'm spitting.
Connecting numbers arranged I'm admitting.
Stealing, stalking my smitten.
The matrix was easy, just collision,
the real deal is severe...

Just as you think what a genius comment.
I am glad that I have got it.
Like an antenna from sender to spender.
Return to the mender. You'd better believe it.
Pattern of the dance all programmed up to see,

Computer's habit, my remedy.
But although there are haters,
and people who breathe other ways, I
will save,
every user and lender, corrupt misled
pretender.
From the ashes, escaping new fashions
in the latest maze. Another day.
It's just that it's a nightmare, noone
seems to care.
What I can see, all in double image to
me,
everybody with flair kicks it back in
harmony.
What if everybody else thought they
were me?
A matrix in electricity.
King of the skies, Prince of I don't know
why,
portraying rhythm slayer until the day I
die.

Part three. With me everytime, all the
while.

Rule one, take heed, the information
that I give you
is all that you will need.
Never taking shit from anyone is what I
believe.
Acid is real life, it is the real thing
but please don't ask me to decide, you
are the ride.
Unsubstantial chemistry, how you slide,
take a look,
A wild time unavailable most days.
Coincide this with your pace.
We all interlace reality to our face.
Perfection. Surely, meditated grace. Rule
two, bass.
Love of life besides love of life, music is a
knife.
Anything I can say can be nice or as
cheap as rice.
Rule three, this ain't the law.
What I saw before, easy but sometimes
crippling
you're listening.
The errors of my ways are showing,
you know that I back everyday,

Extreme saying to play. Alternative
places sting.
I may sing. Coincidental we bring
past troubles and the future on a wing.
Highly fashioned resolution mediating
past display.
No key is ever relevant without the
code,
three beats. Is it as you grow old?
Time holds the fourth as only it unfolds.
Classic battles role bold, a language
rhythmically sold.
The excellent story left in affray,
while anybody has the right to portrait.
Energy everlasting evoked,
Love reckons higher than smoke.
Versions cook, foundations shook,
let me make this clear,
enthusiastic visions so severe.
Treacherous philistines I never believe,
now that I have found how to breathe.
Endeavouring melodies never are
for you to have to read.
Not knowing if it's dark or light,
I don't know if it's wrong or right.

Day or night time my eyes shine,
Psychedelically bright.
Neutral, terminal effects to my brain
and my life. A copy of another bubble,
dilated to fit like skin tight.
The whiteness in my timing, delicately
spiralling.
On the wall only chaotic scrolling
revisited are calling. Honoured just like
literature or statistics, cosmic misfits in
business.
If you are not offended by salvation
and how it tries to manipulate.
To see what's left behind look to the
skies
and interpret.
It still scares the sh*t out of me
everytime,
when it's in my face.
Being straight, am I unequipped? At
this pace, I shall zip.
First sign blues, so confused, always
awakening
I'm shaken.
I'll take, the quickening of the bassline

quaking the race.
See what the method, one, has done to you,
left you gagged and abused.
Illuminated virtual blunts look so amused.
As you closed your eyes animals turned surprised.

Skin I'm in, polyphonic psychedelic, trailing to win.
Treasures dearly buried, steadily thin, evenly narrow the eyes in the sky so readily taint
virtuous reasons, some faint. Again.
Virginal horizons hang tight to the frame,
coincidental passions lighting the way, our specialist rage.
Known by the way that still intimidation plays, correction of day. Events at hand in relay, with nothing less or more to say. I begin. These ideas stretch from being ill to affirmative.

Thoughts mature through letters and confirm it is.
Seven level lights, transposing what lights with
dignity might be displayed, reversing what is right.

Let music be the medium of our transcendental conversation. Life follows the observation,
playing on behalf of revolution, revelation.

On occasion a skill of indeed darkness will bring such light.
Techniques for the hearing, techniques for the sight.
Tendencies are drawn tight, it's not the falling that matters, it's the height.
Rational mechanics adjust the platters.
I thought that it had happened many years ago.
A million raps left to burn in the snow.
When I awoke I just had to know,

time and space so small across forever
will glow.
The public, only what I say is what I
think is right,
across that broadband, demi-semi-
quavers
together are bright.
I have a dream, we all know that the
dream is right
for my audience, allow me, I will for
sight.
The microphone issue, and now the
best,
searching cyclic tests, spaced by
defining breadth.
Only to offer, from this crest
substantially considered quests.
Crafty doubts, bequeathed debt of near
zero effect.
This is the future coming straight at
your life.
A sound here to root you
and keep you surprised.

I say that I've got to chill, and I will

just waiting for the force that leaves me
still.
How much do I need a computer? And
again,
transcendental boundaries will not
leave me insane
in the game. How many styles can you
name?
Even though you are just a link in the
chain
governed by your life or controlling
what you can with your brain, sounds
lead to images,
don't break but play the plain.
Creator of a passage through any
dubious terrain
from microphones through speakers
comes my claim.
You should know what the humans
have done.
Reinterpreted the system until we are
prisoners,
Believed in the dreams that rely on and
listen to us,

Ordained even in nature before us the
same.
The World to entertain.
The time and place are all unmeaning
in this wasted space that contains my
scheming.
Figuring whether it's fine, doesn't play
on my mind,
early in the morning it's back to the
grind.
Social interest won't erase any means
set in play,
converging array. Relaying the facts
that stay
keeping me a slave, to this very day.
Disintegrating muse moves in it's wake
reassuring is the distance that we make.

Take for example the shakes of the bass
collated
reflected meanings of the finest taste.
Original glow of deserted echoes
remain apparent

undefined reasons in torment are scattered.
However battered similarities win, but in the fortune of loss are shattered.
So intimate yet individually patterned.
Sober emotion in depth quite constantly reckoned.
Kisses a final breath away from the body
nurturing into death as if it were a hobby.

He trusts me and I trust him, that's the way it is,
friends to the end.
Dreams are like a telephone, or internet access,
the 'trend'.
On the first day there were cars, on the second there is drink, on the third there was petrol,
on the fourth television. Do you need a link?
On the fifth day was music, and it rocks!
On the sixth is clothes, hats and socks,

on the seventh we forgive. It's a vibe.
I don't need to lie. As you are alive, the
truth survives. Imagination running
wild, why try?

We send all our answers deep into
space,
there is a faith. A trans-orbital place.
Are you told or do you know?
So as the race flows are you quick or
are you slow?
Unidentified source of structure one
day will be so,
I ain't aiming to sound patronising
although you should know.
Can you listen to this and not feel the
same flow?
Do you feel the juice? The journey of
the news?
With each inhale comes the deadly
burning of
paper enthused.
Superhighway in cruise control, well,
meet this vapour. Supremely friendly
and harmless

to the senses in a matter relentless.
Fractional thesis to go, drum and bass will show.
Don't borrow this, it's close for those that know,
superior collections thrown in a row, jungle techno in the summer,
jungle techno in the snow, for basslines that are low
but never corroding the dislocated abode.
This is a story about a man with a plan who fell into a jam, waking up from a beautiful
dream exactly sets the scene.
Feeling abruptly corrupt, in his mind he's had enough.
He aspires to get rid of the scheme and live like he can. Seeing through
things ain't no surprise for this hardcore fan.
Delivering appealing techno to the gang,
arranged gram by gram.

But now the waiting is over, a toxic plot thickens.

Along comes a breakbeat, a scratch that blends with it's collision,

the freshest of decisions. High voltage will oversee this flailing rhapsody of melody.

No politician will ever understand how this was all planned.

Penned in the frame by a master of the game.

No TV news reporter will ever be named

for reporting the claim that shares the most fame.

No individual underneath the revealed truth

need under sell the scoop.

Positive proof and nothing to loose, everything to gain, genius loop.

Some of my records are old, some of them are new,

the important thing is I know what they can do.

Paint a pretty picture for my homies
and the crew.
Professional listening focused and in
view.
How would anyone stop? Dancers and
their moves,
Everyone has a chance to prove,
one World under a groove.
All I need is to keep this extra length
discussion
improving, so bombastic nobody is
loosing.

Now that you have had a taste, let us
lay
what is dead to waste.
All lines that lead to a singularity of
course
are the case.
If you wish, follow this, the show, the
lyrics

of which you may never know.
The words of which will grow upon
the palm of any poor fellow.
The show is but to gloat, light is afloat,
forever mellow.
Cautious ambiguous make play
on whatever singles us.
Nocturnal, the occasional shadow of
diabolical trust.

Fin.

Printed in Great Britain
by Amazon